By **TONY R. JACKSON**

Copyright© 2021 by Tony Jackson

All rights reserved. No part of this book may be reproduced or used in any manner without written permission of the copyright owner except for the use of quotations in a book review.

ISBN 978-1-7374047-6-7

www.iPadYourMoney.com
www.TheRealMoneyCoach.com

Published by: Write Angles Publishing

TABLE OF CONTENTS

ACKNOWLEDGEMENTS	7
FOREWORD	9
PREFACE	13
INTRODUCTION: WHERE IT ALL BEGAN	15
CHAPTER 1: MY FINANCIAL EDUCATION	21
CHAPTER 2 - THE RISKS AND REWARDS OF THE STOCK MARKET	41
CHAPTER 3: WHAT YOU DON'T KNOW CAN BANKRUPT YOU	57
CHAPTER 4: LIVING BENEFITS - CHRONIC, CRITICAL, & TERMINAL ILLNESS	73
CHAPTER 5: YOUR LIFE, YOUR LEGACY	87
CHAPTER 6: PROTECT YOUR LEGACY…LEGALLY	103
CHAPTER 7 - PULLING IT ALL TOGETHER… STEP BY STEP	117
BONUS: THREE THINGS YOU SHOULD KNOW	129

DEDICATION

To my wife, Alisa, thank you for encouraging me to finally author this book, and for believing in me.

ACKNOWLEDGEMENTS

I would like to acknowledge all of the teachers and mentors who have imparted their knowledge and wisdom into me. I would like to extend my gratitude to the many clients who have entrusted me over the years... some of which have loaned their stories to benefit the readers of this book.

Disclaimer
This book was written for informational purposes only. It should not be taken as tax, legal, or investment recommendations or advice to purchase any financial product or implement any financial strategy without consulting a qualified tax, legal, and financial professional as it relates to your personal situation.

Although each story contained in this book is true, the names, location, and other details have been changed to protect the privacy and confidentiality of those involved.

FOREWORD

by Dr. George C. Fraser

> "A good man leaves an inheritance to his children's children."
>
> — PROVERBS 13:22

My good friend Tony Jackson's *"Increase, Protect and Dominate Your Money* is one of the best written and most prescriptive books I've read in quite a while on the well-worn subject of wealth building. Using powerful bullet points, stories, and insightful wisdom, the book is written from the heart, mind, body, spirit, and personal experiences of the author…plus years of research, reading, and thought as an effective leader in this space.

"*I.P.A.D. Your Money"* is a quick read, but it is at the same time revealing, prescriptive, instructive, and sobering. If you are at all curious about what it takes to succeed in the money game and sustain it in these most trying times, Tony has compiled, edited, and creatively added to some of the best stories, strategies, and tactics available. His book is a rich source of insights and solutions. And yes, it's a great year-round read and a wonderful reference. Start now; there is no time to waste. Black America has a lot of catching up to do. Thank you, Tony Jackson, for this masterwork. You will help so many people get on the right track with unlimited opportunities for financial freedom.

There are unlimited opportunities for wealth creation for Blacks in America despite the inherent obstacles, but you must be able to see the trends and apply the principles that are the building blocks of success. Only then will the opportunities come into focus and be within your reach. As an optimist I see hope and promise everywhere, and so does Tony, but while looking, I have also seen the darkness, the weaknesses, and despair that can be so crippling.

These things do not frighten me, however; they only inspire me to do more. That's because the most important and beautiful thing my research did for me was to illuminate the common threads that tie us all together and have kept us sane and productive for nearly four hundred years. Can Tony say all of this in one book? Judge for yourself. Read on or just thumb through the chapters. I believe that once you've digested a small sampling, you will want the whole message. In fact, I'm counting on it.

Our potential, you see, is more magnificent than even I had dared imagine, but we must…

Stay the course

The ship of life sails at sea in search of life

As captains of our fate, we must steer the course confident

our inner compass will always be true

The seas will be stormy but, stay the course

Your scope will view danger, but stay the course

You will be tempted to change direction, but stay the course

Your crew may threaten mutiny, but stay the course

Stay the course and you will land on an island where no one else has landed

It is there you will build your paradise.

DR. GEORGE C. FRASER
AUTHOR, SPEAKER, ENTREPRENEUR
CEO, FRASERNET, INC.

PREFACE

Hello, I am Tony Jackson

I have a degree in accounting and over 25+ years of financial services experience. I've always been a numbers person; but at the same time, and more importantly, I've always been a client-focused advisor, agent, and financial coach. My twenty-five years of studying, reading books, going to seminars, attending webinars, and constant learning will translate to the best financial advice you will ever receive. I'm also an ordained minister who takes pride in helping and serving people. In this industry, I've seen a lot of different things; but I consistently maintain a sense of integrity that has kept me focused. I am a firm believer that given the opportunity to design a plan, policy, or path, we should *always*, 100% of the time, structure it for the client's maximum benefit.

WHY THIS BOOK MATTERS

THE PROBLEM

The purpose of this book is to address issues pertaining to financial miseducation head on and introduce reasonable, understandable tools to fix it.

The main problem is that many people do not have a financial strategy in place, a strategy that will help them properly save for things like college education, family emergencies, and retirement. Most people are simply not saving enough during their working years.

The next problem is people living from paycheck to paycheck whether they are making $1,000 a month or $100,000 a month. In fact, The Wall Street Journal reported that 78% of people are living from paycheck to paycheck. This disturbing cycle has a significant impact in our latter years because people are entering retirement unprepared, underfunded, and without an understanding of the impact of taxes.

INTRODUCTION: WHERE IT ALL BEGAN

Growing up, I can't recall really wanting for anything. My dad worked in a factory for 38 years, and my mom worked at the hospital until she was no longer able due to a disability. My hard-working parents provided well for me and made sure I was taken care of. I didn't know lack or need and will always be thankful for that. It wasn't until it was time for me to go to college that my perspective of my family's money situation hit home.

I really wanted to attend Howard University in Washington, D.C. I had done the research, and my mind was made up. Howard had one of the top accounting programs in the country, and for some reason, I had always dreamt of living there. Thinking back, it was really because of all the federal job opportunities readily available.

Eventually, reality caught up to me. Howard was an out-of-state school and a private institution, so the expenses would be immense. That was the first time I realized that my parents really couldn't afford it. Although I wasn't really hurting for anything, my parents just didn't make enough money. They hadn't saved for their own retirement, let alone have the resources to send me to a school halfway across the country. In short, there was no way my parents could afford to send me to Howard.

By the time of graduation, Dad was retired and Mom was on disability. Fortunately, I received an academic scholarship to attend Western Michigan University, my second choice. My situation was not unique. Just like my parents, many people spend their adult years working around the clock, making just enough to survive; not living, just surviving. Then, they find themselves at retirement age or nearing retirement and are simply unprepared.

A PASSION FOR PLANNING

The year was 1995. I was out of college and had secured a *good* job, as did my wife Alisa, who was expecting our daughter. That's when my mom passed away. I remember sitting in the funeral home with my dad and uncle, who was more like a brother. At that moment my family was informed that my mom had six life insurance policies, but none of them would pay out. I made eye contact with my uncle then turned to my dad and told him I'd pay for the funeral. He looked up with tears in his eyes and said, "No, you won't. That's my wife." With tears streaming down his face he added, "If I have to borrow money on my house, you will not pay for your own mother's funeral." And there it was. That was my first real, personal experience with life insurance. I could not help thinking, "How many more people are like them?" This is one of the biggest reasons I am passionate about life insurance and retirement planning.

My parents did not know what they were getting, and there are so many misguided people just like them. We've all seen the ads on TV and the flyers in the mail or our email inboxes. "Everyone will be accepted!" "Invest in this and this…" It's the old bait and switch, and so many people fall prey to it. We see these advertisements, but most people don't know what they're actually being offered. The internet is inundated with people's opinions about things, and the noise can be ridiculously distracting, not to mention confusing as far as who to believe or not. Well, that stops now…with this book.

THE OLD TYPICAL SOLUTIONS

The typical solutions come from two different financial professionals with two very different agendas. One is from the world of financial advisors, whose primary focus is assets under management. They are the ones who, regardless of how much you make, still make money off your money.

Then you have insurance agents. Shockingly, for many of us, life insurance was once not even available. Outside of small burial policies, major life insurance companies did not offer coverage to African Americans and other minority communities until the late 1950's. Today, many people have a negative mindset toward life insurance because of prior experiences. Believe me, I felt the same way after my mother passed away.

This is all very concerning. However, by the end of this book, you'll see how these two very different financial paths, and very different approaches, can merge together. Merging the concepts can create a winning solution for your financial future, for you, your family, and generations to come. That's what this book is about.

THE REAL SOLUTION: HOW I HAVE CHANGED THE GAME

Many of the concepts you will see in this book were first introduced to me many years ago in a book called *Everything Wall Street and the IRS Doesn't Want You to Know*. It wasn't on anyone's best-seller list, and quite possibly didn't even have an ISBN number. However, the knowledge I gained from that little book was transformational and eye opening. It showed just how many little-known options benefit people. I was introduced to concepts I had never heard of before. In this book, you will get the benefit of my years practicing these little-known trade secrets. Sadly during my years in this business, I've seen too many times where people had fish fries to raise money (that's what people used to do), GoFundMe campaigns, and retired living off of very little. They may have received funds from their social security, or maybe a small pension, but not much more.

Nine out of ten Americans don't know about the life-elevating financial strategies you'll learn about in this book. And that fact is why I have personally made financial coaching my ministry, my passion, and my responsibility. Whether you are from the hard knocks of life, the middle class, or the rich and famous, everyone needs to know these things exist. That's why this book is important.

HOW WILL YOU BENEFIT?

First, I will equip you with tools that will protect you from things like stock market crashes, taxes, and the spend-down process. Another benefit is understanding that there are allowances within the IRS tax code that provide tax-free access to your money. It doesn't matter whether you need it to pay for college or make a down payment on a home, or ultimately use it for retirement. These strategies are perfectly legitimate and are found right in the IRS tax code (Section 26).

They allow you to accumulate money and then take that money out tax-free.

In this book, you will learn strategies that will put you in a great position so you will not outlive your money. The goal is to no longer have to stress about having enough money to retire.

LET'S GET STARTED

All misinformation, miseducation and misconceptions stop with this book. You are a few hours away from the same knowledge that legendary business owners, Walt Disney, James Cash (JC) Penny, Ray Kroc (McDonalds), and countless other families have known for generations. When you finish reading this book, all you have to do is act.

The statement I hear most is, "I wish I would have known this years ago." The good news is; you can start today. There's a proverb that says, "The best time to plant a tree was 20 years ago. The 2nd best time - today." You've waited long enough. Now it is time to increase, protect, and dominate your money. This book is not simply about life insurance or retirement planning. It is about changing your family tree into an orchard of prosperity. It's about creating and maintaining generational wealth.

If you want to speak to me directly, please visit www.IPADAppointment.com to schedule a phone appointment with me today. Let's get started.

CHAPTER 1: MY FINANCIAL EDUCATION

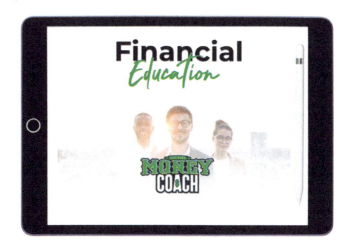

MUSIC, MONEY, AND MARRIAGE - A LOVE STORY

I attended Fruitport High School, located outside of Muskegon, Michigan. Fruitport is about 30 miles west of Grand Rapids. Thinking back on my high school experience, I must admit that it was awesome. I was the classic high achiever, both in sports and academics. Despite being one of only two African Americans in my class, I was voted class president all four years.

In my sophomore year, I took a business class and really liked the accounting portion. So, I enrolled in the advanced accounting class at the county vocational center. Truth be told, it was also an opportunity for me to be around more black kids at Muskegon High School. That's where I met Mr. Les Matthews who taught advanced accounting at the vocational school.

Mr. Les Matthews was a laid-back man from Fremont, Michigan with an off sense of humor. He always told bad jokes. Comedy might not have been his strong suit. However, he really cultivated a love for accounting within me. He wasn't bad at giving practical advice either. I will never forget his biggest tip: *Before you marry, look at the mother and grandmother. That's what you're marrying.* I can truly say that after 29 years of marriage, fortunately for me, he was spot on!

Deciding to take Mr. Matthew's accounting class was a turning point in my journey. I loved it. It was there that I realized that numbers were going to be my thing. By the time I graduated high school, I had already finished one year of college accounting. Although I really wanted to go to Howard, my parents simply couldn't afford it. My mom was 38 and my dad was 45 when I was adopted, so by the time I was of college age, Daddy was already beyond retirement age. He was actually receiving workers' compensation, and Mama was recieving disability benefits. They were living check to check, but I never wanted for anything; I was well provided for. As mentioned, I had no idea about their financial situation until it was time for me to go to college.

I accepted an Academic scholarship to Western Michigan University and was ready for business. I would arrive early on campus, briefcase in hand. In the fall semester of 1986, I went to the student union, the spot where all the students hung out. Just like vultures hovering over fresh meat, the first thing you noticed were credit card companies lined up in front. It wasn't long before I fell into the credit card lair myself. I got a Sears credit card and was ready to make some purchases.

I charged a 300-watt, dual cassette stereo. It was equipped with speaker stands; you could take the cover off and see the subwoofer. The youth of today would have no idea what I'm talking about. Trust me, this thing was serious party-time equipment. I was the most popular freshman in the dorm because I could rock the party.

I still had the stereo after college, and it came with me to my first apartment in Jackson, Michigan. May 6th, 1991 came around, and my beautiful girlfriend, Alisa, of 4 years came over. I had the stereo plugged into the outlet so that when she turned on the light switch, our song would play: *Here and Now,* by Luther Vandross… real grown-folks music that would seal the deal. At that moment, I proposed to her, with the stereo playing in the background. The rest, as they say, is history.

Oh yes, and I was still paying for the stereo. You read that right. I was still paying for the stereo that I bought in 1986. Here it was five years later, and it still wasn't paid for. This scenario is not a unique one, unfortunately. The truth is financial education isn't something most of us get at home, church, or school. It's not even taught in accounting classes. For most people, the tools of financial education simply aren't available in their environment. Our parents do the best with what they have, but we can only teach someone else what we know ourselves. So, where do we learn this important information? I challenge you to think about it. I don't know of any place with a consistent program that delivers financial education as a necessary foundation.

CALLING OUT THE CRISIS

Financial literacy is an issue that should command our attention because many Americans are not adequately organizing finances for their education, healthcare and retirement.
— RON LEWIS, FORMER UNITED STATES REPRESENTATIVE

There is a financial crisis gripping the country today. It affects all types of households from the poor to the supposedly affluent. According to The Wall Street Journal, 78% of Americans are living from paycheck to paycheck regardless of income. This financial crisis is the result of a lack of financial education.

Understandably, the world of financial education is vast. You don't know what you don't know. Unfortunately, there are plenty of legitimate reasons why we do not know much about the financial sector and how it affects our lives. Still, I don't believe in letting ignorance be a crutch. Just because my parents didn't know about certain tools doesn't mean I can take a lazy approach to my own knowledge. I feel it is my responsibility to educate myself and then pass it on to others.

First, let's address what's going on with debt. Why are so many individuals barely surviving on their incomes to the point that being fired from their jobs would mean losing everything within a few months or even weeks? There are three major roadblocks that prevent us from achieving our financial objectives:

1. The impact of debt and the lack of a plan to eliminate it
2. The failure to create and live by a spending plan
3. Not understanding or taking advantage of the time value of money

Perhaps these roadblocks affect you or have been barriers in the past. If any of them do apply, there is nothing to be ashamed about. The first step to doing anything better is realizing the need for change in the first place. Also, I wholeheartedly believe that when we know better, we can do better, so it all starts with first addressing the issues.

These roadblocks can stifle financial freedom both individually and collectively. For example, someone can understand how debt works and still fail to take advantage of a functioning budget. Likewise, you can be an awesome budgeter and understand the importance of differentiating between wants and needs. Still, if you lack an understanding of the time value of money, you could be budgeting far less money than you will need in the future.

The significance of these roadblocks should not be underestimated. Tackling one element and then the other is a start. It begins with a discussion and a very important dialog many households should be having. We're going to do that here. If there is no better time than today, then let's count today as day zero and never look back. Financial education exposes a pathway to making better choices that begin today and continue through generations.

START A DEBT ELIMINATION PLAN

Becoming rich is hard. Staying broke is hard. Choose your hard.

— ERIC WORRE

According to debt.org, personal debt among Americans has reached an alarming level. The statistics show:

- More than 189 million Americans have credit card debt

- The average credit card holder has at least four cards
- On average, each household carries $8,398 in credit card debt
- Total U.S. consumer debt is at $13.86 trillion

Even in my own situation, I didn't know how much the 300-watt stereo would ultimately cost me or how long it would take me to pay it off by just making the minimum payment every month. Not to mention the opportunity cost (the money I could have saved or invested instead).

If a thought like opportunity cost doesn't typically occur to you when it comes time to make purchases, don't feel bad. It's a concept that most people, including financial professionals, overlook all the time. In short, an opportunity cost represents the amount of money you could have invested or accumulated with an alternate option. For example, had I decided not to purchase the stereo, instead of needing money to pay the stereo's bill, I would have had extra money that could be used to invest in something or put into a savings account.

The purpose of this book is not to highlight what you don't know, but to reveal what you need to know to help you enjoy a better financial situation. So, if you find yourself drowning in debt as you read this book, there is good news. You can get out of debt. There are primarily three popular ways to eliminate debt.

THE AVALANCHE METHOD

What gets people in debt generally isn't the amount initially borrowed, but the interest. Interest rates can eat up a budget if you don't have a plan for paying down the initial principle that was borrowed. Higher interest rates make paying off the initial debt much harder, especially if you're only making the minimum payments.

The avalanche method is a method to pay off the debt with the highest interest rate first. After paying off the first debt, you take that payment and move to the next highest interest-bearing debt. You continue this process until all your debts are paid in full. The advantage of this method is that mathematically it is the most efficient in terms of overall interest paid and the time it takes to become debt free. The challenge is that it sometimes takes a long time before you see substantial progress. For someone who needs motivation by seeing progress, this could be a challenging approach to stick with.

THE SNOWBALL METHOD

The snowball method, however, takes the opposite approach. It allows you to see progress sooner by paying off your smallest debt first regardless of the interest rate. By paying off the smaller debts first and then moving to the next smallest debt, you will experience emotional victories along the way. This can be exciting and motivating as you continue your road to be debt free.

If going from having ten creditors down to seven or five helps you keep your mind on the big picture, it could help relieve that sense of never-ending debt that often discourages many people from trying to eliminate debt in the first place. Small victories can be just what you need to stay motivated and focus on making better spending decisions.

THE DEBT ROLL-UP METHOD

This method is very similar to the snowball method but may be best suited for those who enjoy numbers, perhaps spreadsheets, or even a little friendly competition with yourself. Each of your debts are given a score; your objective is to pay the debt with the lowest score first and then roll that payment into paying off the debt with the next lowest score. The score for each debt is determined by taking the balance of each debt and dividing it by the minimum payment. For example, a $200 debt with a minimum payment of $20 would have a score of 10 ($200/$20 = 10).

Whether you choose the avalanche, snowball, or roll-up method, the most important thing is to take action. Also, don't fret about choosing the right or wrong method. There really is no right or wrong way to do it unless you don't do anything at all. Maybe you think the avalanche method will be beneficial because you have some really high-interest credit cards. You might choose the snowball approach for the emotional victories. Perhaps using a combination of the different approaches is appealing. The point is to start. Begin the debt free journey today, and you will be surprised at how quickly you become debt free.

START A BUDGET

More people should learn to tell their dollars where to go instead of asking them where they went."
– ROGER BABSON, EARLY 20TH CENTURY ENTREPRENEUR, FOUNDER OF WEBBER AND BABSON COLLEGES

I have often said that if you don't tell your money where to go (budget), then it will go wherever it wants to. Having a budget, or spending plan, is something that we all know is beneficial, but most people don't have one. I get it. It can be intimidating and discouraging when the numbers don't quite add up or we get off course. Some even avoid making a budget because doing so might show them that they have less than they thought and that is a hard pill to swallow.

Budgeting is like learning to walk or to ride a bike. When we fall down, we get back up and keep trying until we have mastered the skill. It gets easier over time. It does take setting an intention and taking the initiative, but over time it gets easier. Deciding not to work with a budget won't remedy the situation. Remember that ignorance is not the solution. Some people refuse to look at their bank accounts because they don't like the numbers they see. Can you imagine how difficult it might be to get an idea of how much you're working with if you're afraid to even look at the account? Budgeting does not need to feel intimidating. Actually, the more you are aware of your budget, the easier maintaining one becomes.

Here are some steps to consider when making a budget.

1. **Determine your income.** How much money do you bring home from work, your business, investments, or any other sources of income? This is vital because you have to know what you are working with. I promote multiple streams of income by the way. If you currently have just one sole source of income, that's fine. As you become more financially aware of your spending, saving, and budgeting habits, hopefully you will make better decisions that will eventually free up how you spend your time as well. With more time and better education, you might find yourself inspired to pursue other income avenues such as gig work, freelance opportunities, or entrepreneurship. Having more than one source of income not only provides more resources to tackle your debt but can help also alleviate the stress that causes many people to get into huge debt situations in the first place.

2. **Decide how much you're going to save.** This step requires you to be realistic. Making this determination defies the conventional process. In most cases,

people leave saving to the end and it becomes whatever is left over. I believe we must be more intentional about our savings. It is not easy. I have struggled with it over the years. Many people have, but that doesn't make it impossible. You can do it. Think of an aggressive, doable number you can aspire to. Saving doesn't have to be like facing an insurmountable mountain; it should be a goal that you realistically see yourself achieving. The most important takeaway here I want to emphasize is that saving should not be optional. Make having a savings goal part of your budget as much as spending. *I had a seventy-year-old client who saved $1,000 after learning the strategies I shared with her. She'd never learned them. She was absolutely ecstatic. If she can do it, you can do it.*

3. **List your fixed expenses.** Most people think "fixed" expenses are those things that have the same payment every month. In this book, we're going to look at fixed expenses differently. I want you to think of fixed expenses as the things you have to pay, such as your mortgage (or rent), utilities, food, transportation to work, and other essentials. Many of these items may vary from one month to the next, but they are vital for your survival.

4. **List your variable expenses.** These expenses add up to the discretionary spending we all do that is not vital to our existence. Oftentimes, these are the things that bring us joy and are part of our lifestyles. I do not

advocate that you completely eliminate these things, but you should be aware of them and exercise control and discipline. Also, be aware of the items listed in your fixed expenses. Make sure that you have honestly categorizing them. It might be tempting to assign an expense as necessary, but be sure that it doesn't belong among the variables if it's truly not required for survival. Examples of variable expenses include streaming services, entertainment, compulsive shopping, etc.

5. **Ongoing management.** Once you have written out your income and total expenses, you now know what you are working with (i.e. your bottom line). Do any of these numbers take you by surprise? Even at a brief glance, do you see where you may need to make some adjustments in your spending? Or maybe the bottom line gives you the little boost you needed to start that side business you've been thinking about. You must decide how you are going to manage your budget. Establish a regular time when you are going to review your spending plan on a weekly and monthly basis. I suggest a day and time when stress and distractions are low, and you can commit to consistently. For instance, reviewing your budget in between commercial breaks of your favorite television show might not be the best time for your concentration. If you feel most productive in the morning, maybe set aside a moment on a Saturday morning before jumping into the day's activities. This time should also include tracking. There are many apps and programs that can assist you with daily

recording. Some features include linking directly with your bank so that it manages deposits and withdrawals automatically. Some even allow you to categorize your spending so you know if you're over the spending goal in a particular category. Find one that works for you and use it!

THE TIME VALUE OF MONEY

I think people don't understand compound interest because typically no one ever explains it to them and the level of financial literacy in the US is very low.
– JAMES SUROWIECKI, JOURNALIST AT THE NEW YORKER

Understanding the time value of money is very important because it can either work against you, as in the case of debt, or it can be used in your favor when investing. The time value of money suggests that today's dollar has the potential to grow in the future (through investments). The contrasting position is when it comes to debt. If you spend $20 to buy new headphones on credit, but it takes you a couple of billing cycles to pay it off, your dollar is worth less.

In today's instant gratification world, we are often looking for those "get rich quick" opportunities. Yes, they do exist, but the worthwhile ones are rare and usually come with a higher risk than most people are willing to assume. Slow and steady wins the race. Albert Einstein understood this when he said, "Compound Interest is the eighth wonder of the world. He who understands it, earns it; he who doesn't pays it." There are some basic rules you should be aware of as it relates to the time value of money. Understanding how compound interest works can help shift your perspective toward spending and saving. Additionally, there are some other factors to keep in mind when it comes to the time value of money.

COMPOUND INTEREST

Compounding interest is a powerful concept that will significantly improve your investment returns. Compounding interest allows an investment the opportunity to increase exponentially because your money earns interest on both the principal and on the prior returns. Time is one of the most important factors that determines the benefits you receive. Compound interest makes the case for investing your money into interest-producing commodities so your money grows as time passes. Think about instruments like high-interest savings accounts, stocks with growth potential, and cash value life insurance. The younger you are, the greater your advantage for compounding interest working in your favor. Saving just $100 a month for 50 years will grow into a very nice little cushion for retirement. However, people of all ages can benefit from compounding interest. Of course, the more years the interest accumulates, the more the money grows. However, starting today will still make a difference in a few years.

The most important tip when it comes to compound interest is to leave it alone. Compound interest works when the value is allowed to build over time. This means taking money out of your interest-earning account for non-emergencies could really stifle the potential for your dollar's growth.

THE RULE OF 72

If you are like most people, you love to see how your money is growing. Getting a rough estimate of how much time it will take to double your money also helps to keep you motivated and consistent in your saving habits. Rule of 72 is an easy formula to calculate how long it will take for your investment to double in value. Take the number 72 and divide it by the annual interest rate you are receiving. The resulting number is the estimated number of years that your investment will double. Keep in mind that every rule has its exceptions. Although Rule of 72 is a common way to plan investment returns, numbers can get slightly skewed. The assessment works best when the fixed return rates are between 6% and 10%. Still, it's a great tool when evaluating different investment opportunities at a glance.

AVERAGES DON'T WORK

Most investments advertise average market returns. For example, ABC investment has averaged a 10% return over the last ten years. That appears to be a very attractive rate for an investor. What this statement doesn't account for, however, is the year-to-year data. People think they understand averages, but they don't. For the lack of a better alternative, I understand the necessity of providing average returns, but the reality is that averages don't work in real life. In terms of temperature, if someone were to ask you, "How's the weather in the spring?" you'd automatically think in terms of the average temperature, but this does not take into account the fact that the temperature can vary from one day to the next or even morning to evening in the same day.

Therefore, if you dress for the average temperature, most of the time, you're going to be either too hot or too cold. Financial growth operates in a very similar way. Your money doesn't operate in average growth. It operates in specifics as it relates to gains and losses. While announcing average returns may sound attractive in advertising, it leaves out the specifics. Negative returns can have a tremendous impact on the actual realized investment returns. Here's an example using $1000 as the starting investment.

	Starting investment $1000.		
	Investment Return	Actual Impact	Balance
Year 1	+ 20%	+ $200	$1,200
Year 2	- 10%	- $120	$1,080
Year 3	+ 10%	+ $108	$1,188
Average Return = + 6.7%			

Advertised as 6.7% return. Here's the misconception it creates.

	Avg. Return	Assumed Impact	Assumed Balance
Year 1	+ 6.7%	+ $67	$1,067
Year 2	+ 6.7%	+ $71	$1,138
Year 3	+ 6.7%	+ $76	$1,214

The use of averages in almost all situations results in an overstatement of reality. In this example, the real rate of return over the three years is 11.8% which is a real-life average of 3.9%.

In the next chapter, you will further discover how negative returns can have a devastating impact on your financial security.

1. Where did you learn about money management?
2. Who are your money mentors/influencers?
3. Do you have a budget and/or debt elimination plan?

To find out more about financial education or to schedule an appointment to speak with me, visit: www.TheRealMoneyCoach.com.

CHAPTER 2 – THE RISKS AND REWARDS OF THE STOCK MARKET

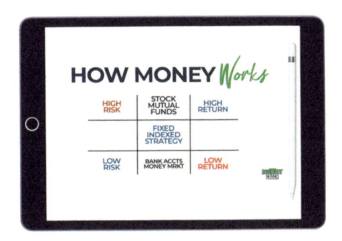

"Hi, Tony Jackson. This is Mrs. Johnson from Richmond. I am just calling to say that I did get the paperwork so I know that my account with you is now valued at $157,685.49. Things are just as you said. It's going up even though the market is volatile because of the virus and all of that. So, I wanted to let you know that I read the statement. I won't be putting any more money in because, as you know, this is an income account for me and I have to withdraw money as I go. So, that's okay with me but I just wanted to let you know that I did get the notice. Thank you very much. Have a good evening. Bye-bye." This is a voicemail transcript from one of my clients during the stock market crash caused by COVID-19.

In July of 2018, I was at a friend's family reunion in South Carolina. It was the typical good old Carolina-style barbeque family reunion: eighties music, dancing, and lots of smiles. What made the biggest impression on me is that this family was financially progressive. Business meetings were always part of their yearly festivities. For this particular year's reunion, I was invited to speak about generational wealth. I used the opportunity to present an abbreviated version of my "Increase, Protect, and Dominate Your Money" presentation. (The full presentation is available at www.ipadyourmoney.com.)

A senior member of the family, Mrs. Johnson, approached me after my presentation. "I want to learn more about protecting my investments," she explained. "Would you be willing to drive to Richmond to meet?" These are the kinds of clients that get me excited about my work. It is one thing to take in information new to you and let it sit. Then, there are the ones who receive new information and act on it. Mrs. Johnson was the latter, and it worked in her favor.

I drove to Richmond to meet with Mrs. Johnson. As we were sitting in the kitchen reviewing her financial portfolio, I explained that although we were in a bull market, which is good for her investments, there were things she could adjust to protect her money in case of a market crash, while still growing her investments. A bull market is the term used to describe a period when the market is going up, and investors are confident it will continue to do so. A "bear" maket, or a declining market, is just opposite. Understandably, at first it was a challenge for her to wrap her mind around the need to make any changes. The economy was in a bull market, and things were looking good. Why be concerned?

After reviewing her financial goals, however, we took some time to analyze all the strategies available to her. Wisely, Mrs. Johnson decided to take my advice on protecting some of her investments from the *unknown*.

You have no doubt heard the common expression, "The only thing in life that is constant is change." Well, the financial markets are no different. Good today does not equate to good tomorrow, as we soon found out with the impact of COVID-19 on the global economy. Not only do the markets change, but they can change swiftly and drastically.

Mrs. Johnson's curiosity led her to begin analyzing her financial security. We are both glad she did. Neither of us had a clue that *the unknown* financial change was just over a year away and would come in the form of a global coronavirus.

The coronavirus was the deadliest pandemic our country has seen in over a hundred years. Furthermore, not only was the pandemic deadly, but it completely devastated millions of financially unprepared families.

The market shifted suddenly and considerably. Everyone was caught by surprise. From big business to small businesses, several industries were affected, and no one was untouched. What looked like an unfortunate, yet controllable virus turned the world on its head. Unanticipatedly, many people had to tap into their savings just to cover basic necessities. This, of course, is good news for people who had savings to fall back on. Unfortunately, many did not.

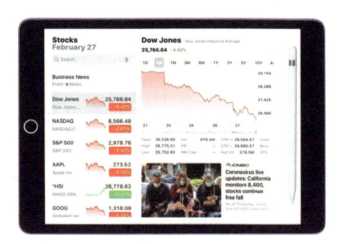

THE PANDEMIC AND THE DREADED PHONE CALL

February 2020 marked the moment of a worldwide pandemic. This is also when the coronavirus made its way into the United States and the financial markets. Stocks plummeted in a free fall. It was the worst stock market crash since 2008.

For folks working in the financial sector, a market crash triggers a flood of unique concerns. At any given moment, it's important to keep an eye on the market and what it's doing, but something of immense influence like the pandemic created a panic like no other. The one thing that most financial advisors dread at moments like this is for the phone to ring. They know that the likely voice on the other end is a client losing their shirt over what's happening in the market. The hopes and dreams of a stress-free retirement are being evaporated with every down tick of the stock market. So, advisors have to somehow assure client after client with conviction that it's okay as they are losing their life savings.

Typically, financial advisors answer with one of the following statements: "Remember you're in it for the long hall", "We've seen this before…", "We can make some adjustments…", "Don't panic…", or the worst-case scenario, "Please leave a message, I'll call you back."

Do any of these responses sound familiar ? Hopefully, you have a respectable, professional advisor handling your portfolio who will be responsive and sensitive to your anxiety. They are out there. Still, even the most experienced advisors might have had a difficult time consoling their clients through this one. And, for good reason. What we all witnessed on a global scale is unlike anything we've experienced in our lifetimes.

What's more, when it comes to money, especially someone's life savings, the assurances are a little harder to grasp. Financial advisors weigh this type of risk in their day-to-day routine. It's essential for average investors to understand certain concepts.

WHAT'S YOUR RISK TOLERANCE?

There's one golden investment rule that you should always keep in mind: never invest money that you can't afford to lose.
— JOSHUA KENNON, THE BALANCE

Risk Tolerance is a term used by financial advisors and stockbrokers as a tool to decide which stocks or mutual funds to place a client's money in. By definition, risk tolerance is the degree of variability in investment risk that an investor is willing to withstand financially.

In layman's terms, risk tolerance is your comfort level with the possibility that you may lose your money. This makes risk tolerance a very important component of investing. There are many ways to measure one's risk tolerance; some are very complex and others are rather simple. For example, let's say on a risk tolerance scale of 1 to 10, 1 is the lowest risk tolerance and 10 is the highest. A person who is at 10 doesn't care at all if he loses every dime of his investment. On the other hand, the person who is at 1 on the scale would rather cut a hole in his mattress and put his money in it rather than take any chance that he might lose a single penny.

In reality, most people fall somewhere in the middle of the scale. I call this the movable middle. If we remove both extremes on the ends of the scale, most people are going to float between a 3 and 7 during their lifetime. Generally speaking, the younger you are the more likely you will fall into the 5-7 range. Conversely, the older you are the more likely you will land into the 3-5 range. However, age is not the only determining factor. An easy way to assess your risk tolerance is by answering three important questions:

1. Where did the money come from?
2. What do you want the money to do for you?
3. When do you want the money to do it?

Unpacking these questions helps to gather the necessary information to determine one's level of risk tolerance for a particular investment. Someone may be more inclined to protect money they've worked hard for versus money they acquired as a gift.

Then, it's important to think about what you want to do with the money, and when you want to do it. Of course, everyone wants their money to grow, but think beyond that. What is your intention for the money - retirement, college savings for your children, a cushion savings account for unexpected expenses like medical bills or home repair? The more candid you are about your money goals, the better your chances of achieving them. Likewise, being upfront about your level of comfortability regarding your investments will help you make wise financial decisions.

Also note that your risk tolerance might differ depending on the investment. For example, my approach to the essential money that I am going to depend on to retire and live off of in my golden years may have a lower risk tolerance than the money I want for discretionary spending like vacations.

STOCK & MUTUAL FUNDS - #10 ON THE RISK SCALE

Unless you can watch your stock holding decline by 50% without becoming panic stricken, you should not be in the stock market.

— WARREN BUFFET

Everyone wants to be a big player on the stock market. After all, saying that you own Apple, Nike, Amazon, or Facebook stock can be pretty impressive… and frankly, it is if you got in at the right time. The optimal word here is "if."

For some, the stock market is an intimidating or complicated land of wonder. So, what is it really? We hear terms like the Dow Jones or S&P 500, but most people really don't have a clue as to what those things are. First, the stock market is a broadly-used term to refer to the collection of markets and exchanges, where the activity of buying and selling shares (ownership) of publicly-held companies occurs. Most notably is the New York Stock Exchange. The value of the shares on the exchange can, and do, fluctuate quite often on a daily basis.

The aforementioned Dow Jones and S&P 500 indexes are simply a grouping of certain companies for valuation and statistical purposes. The Dow Jones is a composite of the 30 largest publicly-traded companies in the US while the S&P 500 expands that number to 500 of the largest publicly traded companies. Because the S&P 500 in essence has a larger sampling, it is a better measurement of the strength of our economy.

The reality is that individual investors account for less than one-third of stock market ownership, and the majority of individual owners are the richest and wealthiest members of our society. Large institutional investors like hedge funds, pension funds, and mutual funds control the market, and they are not looking to share the wealth.

This is what caused the GameStop/Robinhood backlash in March of 2021. Robinhood was making opportunities available to average investors that had been normally reserved for the big institutional investors. Those institutional investors quickly forced Robinhood to shut these opportunities down.

This all means that ordinary individual investors like you and I are left on the outside looking in. Make no mistake, our money is included in the form of 401(k)s, IRAs, brokerage accounts, etc. but we have no control or say so. We can only watch.

Imagine you are standing outside the gates of your favorite amusement park. As you look into the sky, there it is: the rollercoaster with all its curves, twists, ups and downs. The carrier creeps up the track, little by little, until it reaches the highest point. Then suddenly, it drops at a furious speed. The people scream at the top of their lungs. Some scream from the adrenaline rush, but others scream out of fear.

When you are heavily invested in stocks and mutual funds, your money is on that roller coaster. Think about how you personally feel about being on a roller coaster. I have personally never liked them. As I get older, I like them even less. I am certainly not interested in going for a ride on a rollercoaster, not physically or financially.

When we take a look at the performance of the S&P 500 over the last 20 years (1999-2019), it remarkably resembles a roller coaster track. Yes, there are a lot of peaks, but they are offset by huge losses in 2000, 2001, 2002, and 2008. All of this was before the COVID-19 crisis.

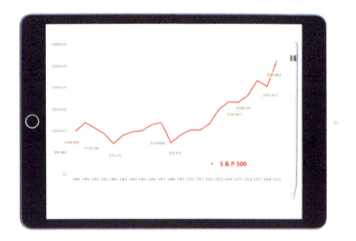

When will the next drop happen? How long will it take to recover? No one knows. Just like Mrs. Johnson didn't know when I met with her in her kitchen.

BANK ACCOUNTS - SAVINGS & MONEY MARKETS - RISK SCALE #1

It is enough that people of the nation do not understand our banking and monetary system, for if they did, I believe there would be a revolution before tomorrow morning.

— HENRY FORD

We have all heard the phrase, "Cash is King." While that may be true in the world of retail, it's a slow death in the world of investing and retirement planning. Although bank accounts are normally very safe and tend to be the fallback position when getting off the financial rollercoaster, they simply do not hold up to the test of time (See the Time Value of Money section from Chapter One).

There is this thing called inflation. The economic definition of inflation is a general increase in prices and the fall in the purchasing value of money. Inflation in April of 2021 was 2.26%. However, according to bankrate.com, the best savings account rate in the nation was a mere 0.57%. Bank accounts provide a very safe haven for our money, but they substantially reduce our buying power. In other words, the cost of living is almost 4 times the rate of our money (2.26/0.57=3.9). For individuals or families looking to save to purchase a home, send their kids to college, or even retire, this is simply not going to work. The numbers don't add up. For those approaching retirement or are currently retired already, it's not much better.

The US Census Bureau estimates that the average person will spend 18 years in retirement. Think about the impact of losing buying power for 18 years. Furthermore, I know many people who have lived in retirement well beyond that average. The number one fear of retirees is they will run out of money. With inflation growing at 4 times the rate of their money in the bank, their fear is real.

THE MOVEABLE MIDDLE - RISK TOLERANCE SCALE 4-6

The four most dangerous words in investing are: 'this time it's different.'

— SIR JOHN TEMPLETON

So, what is the answer? Is there a magic bullet? On the one hand, you have high returns but high risk. On the other hand, there is low risk and low returns. Is there a viable solution for the moveable middle?

The answer is yes, and it is called the fixed index strategy. It is essentially a "have my cake and eat too" type of strategy. Most fixed indexed strategies follow one of the stock market indexes like the S&P 500. When that index increases in value, your account is credited a portion of that increase. However, if that index decreases in value, your account is not impacted negatively at all. Your account stays level.

As the economy grows and stock market values increase, you get to participate in the growth, which ultimately helps to offset the impact of inflation. Not if, but *when* the market crashes, your money and previous gains are all protected. This is exactly what Mrs. Johnson experienced with her account.

There are a lot of details we have to be educated on because not all indexed strategies are the same. Some have different earning caps, participation rates, minimums, and fees. The one you should choose goes back to those three questions mentioned earlier to determine risk tolerance. The power of the fixed indexed strategy provides a workable solution to the issues discussed earlier. See the chart below.

Many financial advisors do not like fixed indexed products. Why? There are two main arguments. The first is that they can outperform the market index. According to CNBC (March 15, 2019), only 8% of fund managers outperformed the S&P 500 over the last 15 years. Unless your financial advisor is in the top 8% of money managers in the entire country each year, you would be better off following the S&P 500 index even with its occasional market corrections (better known as a market crash). Certainly, being in a strategy that eliminates negative returns puts you in a much better situation.

The second argument is typically based on fees. Most people realize that every investment vehicle has some fees. The question becomes twofold: how much are the fees and what am I getting in return for these fees? Forbes magazine warned its readers in a June 2020 article titled, "Small Fees Have a Big Impact on Your Investments." The two fees exposed were mutual fund expenses and financial advisor fees. The bottom line is that these fees tend to line the pockets of the large institutional investors mentioned earlier and the pockets of the money managers. In essence, fees pay the money managers who literally fail 92% of the time to beat the S&P 500 index.

If you are going to pay fees, you should at least get something in exchange. Otherwise, you're only making someone else rich. In exchange for your fees, you should be getting lifetime income and/or guarantees against market loss, critical illness, chronic illness, and perhaps even a death benefit.

The intention here is not to bash financial advisors. I personally know some very good traditional financial advisors who play an important role in long-term financial planning. For the average investor, knowledge of these alternatives do not directly benefit the financial advisor, so they have no incentive to inform you.

Remember that the goal is to expose some alternative concepts that can put you in a better financial position so you are not blindsided by the unexpected.

What is your investment risk tolerance: high risk taker, moderate, or conservative?

Have you ever lost money due to stock market declines?

Are you concerned about the impact of future market crashes on your money?

To learn more about the fixed indexed strategy and how it could be implemented to stabilize your portfolio, book your free financial review today at www.ipadappointment.com.

CHAPTER 3: WHAT YOU DON'T KNOW CAN BANKRUPT YOU

INCOME TAXES AND RETIREMENT

MEET MRS. JONES

Mrs. Jones graduated from Hampton University with a degree in Education and eventually became a public school teacher in Prince George County in Maryland. She absolutely loved her role as an educator. Every day she shaped the lives of future generations, and the kids loved her for it. Her dedication and commitment led to her being honored as teacher of the year. Throughout her career, Mrs. Jones had scores of accolades and a tremendous impact on the students she taught.

Like most teachers, Mrs. Jones participated in the annual enrollment process of selecting her benefits, including the typical things we are accustomed to receiving from our employer: health insurance, dental, and of course retirement. Mrs. Jones followed the recommended course of action by participating in the state teacher pension plan, but she also went above and beyond by also contributing to the optional 403b retirement savings plan. After forty years as a dedicated educator, she finally decided to retire and return home to the Carolinas.

Fast forward to the day I first met Mrs. Jones. I did a presentation at a local church. After the presentation, an older, petite, lady with silvery platinum hair asked me if it were possible to meet and discuss her retirement portfolio. My heart flooded with familiarity because she reminded me of my own mother.

"Of course I can. What's your name, ma'am?"

"Mrs. Jones," she replied with a gentle smile. She was kind natured and continued smiling as we engaged." Mrs.

Jones, ma'am, you remind me of my mother," I said as I began to smile as well.

"Well your mother must be a very nice lady," she replied.

We exchanged contact information, scheduled our appointment, and went on our separate ways. During my meeting with Mrs. Jones I discovered a common situation seen in a lot of people her age. Mrs. Jones started saving early in life, lived a very frugal life, below her means, and did all the things we are told by society we should do to have a healthy retirement. This included stacking away a great portion of her income into the state pension and 403b retirement plans. As a retiree, Mrs. Jones was relentlessly self-sufficient. She had enough money to live comfortably according to the lifestyle she created for herself, and even treat herself from time to time. But as we poured through her financial documentation, she paused, looked me directly in the eyes, and asked in a clear and somber tone, "Tony, why am I paying so much in income taxes?"

MEET MR. BAKER

Mr. Baker lived in Albion, Michigan. It's a small town of about 3,000 people, anchored directly in between Battle Creek and Jackson, Michigan. Armed with a high school diploma, Mr. Baker worked at the town supermarket bagging groceries.

Job opportunities were limited in Albion, so Mr. Baker continued working at the grocery store. In five short years, Mr. Baker went from bagging groceries, then to cashier, and with a few other roles in between, eventually landed the role of the Meat Department Manager.

From time to time, he noticed one particular gentleman, who was not from Albion, buying the best steaks in the supermarket. What made him stand out was that he always wore a suit and tie, and had a certain demeanor of distinction that made him appear wealthy.

On one particular occasion, the gentleman asked Mr. Baker how he enjoyed his job as the manager of the meat department.

"I love it, although I could stand to make a bit more money." Mr. Baker replied laughingly.

The gentleman slid his business card on the counter, grinned and said, "Well, if you're serious about more money, give me a call."

Mr. Baker, who had already imagined himself trading in his white meat apron for a suit and tie, took the card and called him the next day. Within a few weeks, Mr. Baker started his career as an insurance agent. Not long after, he opened his own agency.

As an independent insurance agent, he didn't have access to the traditional retirement plans that most people have while working for the government or in corporate America. However, he was exposed to a wide variety of alternative retirement strategies that aren't offered to traditional employees.

He invested in real estate, other business ventures, mutual funds, and mostly in cash value life insurance. At that time, there were primarily two types of cash value life insurance: whole life and universal life. After over 30 years of service, Mr. Baker retired, and that's when I met him. He eventually transferred all of his insurance policies to me.

I will never forget the day Mr. Baker came to my office. He sat down in front of my desk, spread out the brochure of a beautiful luxury SUV, and made this request: "I am buying this next week. I need $50,000 out of my account." A few days later, he returned to my office to pick up his check… no questions, no paperwork, and no taxes.

THE SIMILARITIES AND DIFFERENCES

Comparing apples to apples, Mrs. Jones and Mr. Baker share a few similarities. They are both Baby Boomers (people born between 1946 and 1964). They are both very frugal and live well below their means. They both have been great savers and had long-term, successful careers. In addition, they were both around 70 years old when I began working with them.

Obviously, there are also differences between these two individuals. They grew up in different parts of the country and had very different educational backgrounds. However, the biggest difference between Mrs. Jones and Mr. Baker is that Mr. Baker understood something early in his career that Mrs. Jones had never been exposed to: the impact of taxes on retirement.

THE THREAT OF TAXES

For most people the biggest threat to their financial security is taxes.

— THE AMERICAN TAX PLANNING INSTITUTE

The impact of taxes on future income is almost never accounted for by financial planners nor by other financial professionals, including many income tax preparers. When we look at the layers upon layers of taxes we each pay, it's easy to understand why most Americans are looking for every possible legal tax deduction we can find. In fact, taxes are the single largest expense item that most working adults will pay in their lifetime. More than your car. More than student loans. Even more than your mortgage. So, to ignore the impact of taxes is the equivalent to an ostrich sticking his head in the sand while the whole world around him is exploding. Today we will pull our heads out of the sand.

We must first understand where our tax dollars are being spent. The four largest budget items for the federal government are 1) Medicare/Medicaid, 2) social security, 3) defense spending, and 4) interest on the national debt. According to the Governmental Accounting Office, these four items account for over 90% of every dollar collected by the Internal Revenue Service (IRS). COVID-19 has had a direct and major impact on three out of four of these top budget items: Medicare/Medicaid, social security, and interest on the national debt.

MEDICARE/MEDICAID

In 2020, there were over 32 million cases of COVID-19 in the United States alone. Data shows that over 35% of the US population are covered either by Medicaid or Medicare. Statistically speaking, this represents a significant portion of the US population. It equates to over 11 million COVID-19 cases potentially covered by the largest government program in the budget. Where is this money going to come from?

SOCIAL SECURITY

Over 50 million people filed for unemployment in 2020. The impact of all that unemployment created a unique burden on the US economy. It meant that 50 million people and their employers did not pay into the social security trust fund. Yet, nationally about 10,000 baby boomers turn 65 every day and they file for Medicare and social security benefits. It's the makings of a perfect financial storm…less money going in the social security trust fund and more money coming out of it. Where is this money going to come from?

INTEREST ON THE NATIONAL DEBT

Due to the economic impact of COVID-19, the US government passed three stimulus packages in 2020 and an additional stimulus package in the first quarter of 2021 as of the writing of this book. These four stimulus packages were designed to boost the economy and provide needed financial relief to the American people. The stimulus package included things like increased unemployment benefits, stimulus checks, and loans for small businesses, etc. However, these four stimulus packages came with a price tag of nearly eight trillion dollars. Here lies the problem. The US had to borrow these funds and thus, increase the national debt. Increased national debt means more taxes to repay the principal and the loan interest. Remember from chapter one, compound interest can work for you or against you. Considering the spike in the need for governmental assistance as a result of the coronavirus disease, that's a hefty ticket to cover. Where is this money going to come from?

WHAT WILL TAXES BE IN THE FUTURE?

"But, in this world, nothing is certain except death and taxes."

— BENJAMIN FRANKLIN

As I outlined above, COVID-19 added fuel to the fire as it relates to taxes. In previous sections, I asked on several occasions, "Where is all this money going to come from?" The answer can be summed up in one word, You! That's right. You, and I shall pay the taxes, is the answer. The US government only has one way to raise revenue and that's through taxation. At some point taxes will increase. In fact, unless Congress acts quickly, the current tax rates are scheduled to increase in 2025. Here's a partial list of the tax benefits that will end in 2025.

- Reduction in personal income tax rates
- Increase in the standard deduction
- Increased childcare credit
- Limits on state and local tax deductions
- Reduction in estate taxes

The argument made for years is that you will be in a lower tax bracket when you retire. You can find plenty of so-called financial gurus on the internet that make this claim. Many retirees, like Mrs. Jones, found out that this is not true at all. In fact, the opposite is their reality. Mr. Baker, however, understood this concept very early in his career.

Retirement accounts are actually low hanging fruit for the IRS. If you don't believe me, try calling your employer's human resource department and ask to withdraw your retirement funds. You will be hit with taxes and penalties to the tune of 40% or more. The government intentionally created these barriers to lock in the funds in the above-mentioned programs. As more people become educated about their options, if too many withdrew their money, there would not be much left to dole out to the Internal Revenue Service (IRS). For all these reasons, we must begin to rethink the issue of taxes.

TAX PREPARATION VS TAX PLANNING

"Always plan ahead. It wasn't raining when Noah built the ark."

— RICHARD CUSHING

Because of the volatility and impact of taxes, we need to begin the process of long-term tax planning just like Mr. Baker did. It is important that we make the distinction between tax preparation and tax planning. Most people are familiar with tax preparation. It is that familiar time of year from about mid-January to mid-April. During the tax season, we often work with tax return preparers to complete our personal and business taxes. The goal is to pay the least amount every year. This is a micro approach to taxes.

Controversially, tax planning is a macro approach. Tax planning seeks to develop strategies that result in the least amount of taxes paid over our lifetime and upon our death. Frankly, we need to take both into account in our approach to taxes. The problem is that oftentimes these two approaches are at odds with one another. This is because we are accustomed to living in the moment. As a result, we simply opt for the short-term gratification of taking certain deductions today and completely ignore the enormous tax burden that awaits us in future. In most cases, this is not an intentional act. Like Mrs. Jones, most of us have not been exposed to this truth until it's nearly too late.

WHICH BUCKET DO YOU WANT?

The avoidance of taxes is the only intellectual pursuit that carries any reward.

— JOHN MAYNARD KEYNES

When it comes to money, especially retirement money, there are three main categories. We will refer to these categories as buckets.

First is the Taxable Bucket. This bucket and its growth are taxed every year. It includes banking products such as checking accounts, savings accounts, money market accounts, certificate of deposits (CD's), and certain investments.

The second bucket is the Tax Deferred Bucket. This bucket and its growth are not taxed until it is withdrawn at a later date such as retirement. It normally includes money that is being held in IRA, 401(k), 403(b), and TSP accounts.

The third bucket is the Tax-Free Bucket. Money placed into this bucket is not taxed while it is growing nor is it taxed when withdrawn. There are very few money vehicles that truly accomplish tax-free status. The two that we are most familiar with are cash value life insurance and a Roth IRA if it is held long enough and meet certain criteria.

SECTION 26 - FOR BETTER OR WORSE

You must pay taxes. But there's no law that says you got to leave a tip.

— MORGAN STANLEY

Before concluding this chapter on taxes, it is important to touch briefly on Section 26 of the Internal Revenue Code (IRC). When it comes to retirement, this section of the IRC determines how your retirement funds will be treated. In fact, 401(k) and 403(b) are actually subsections of Section 26.

There are a few rules to be aware of in particular. The 59 ½ Rule is the tax code that allows the IRS to penalize you an extra 10% on top of the normal tax rate if you take money out of your tax-qualified retirement plan, such as those in the tax-deferred bucket (401(k), 403(b), IRA, TSP, etc.). The Required Minimum Distribution (RMD) Rule is the tax code that requires that you take a certain amount of your money out of your tax deferred bucket in the tax year that you turn 72 years old. If you do not withdraw the required amount, the IRS will impose a 50% penalty on that amount. For example, if that amount is $10,000 and you don't withdraw it, the IRS will send you a bill for $5000. It is worth noting that if you pass away and your beneficiary is someone other than a spouse, those retirement funds will be treated tax wise, much like RMD, regadless of age.

Understand that following these rules does not prevent us from having to pay taxes on all the money, including the principle, that we withdraw from our tax-deferred retirement bucket. In essence then, Section 26 is not necessarily working in our favor. However, there are two rarely used codes hidden in Section 26, which are 72e and 7702. These two codes allow for the accumulation of funds inside of a life insurance policy in the tax-deferred bucket. However, when you withdraw the funds it comes out through the tax-free bucket.

Keep it REAL!

1. Are you concerned about the impact of taxes on your retirement funds?
2. Do you have money in all three buckets: taxable, tax deferred, and tax free?
3. Do you have a long-term tax-free retirement strategy?

Take Action Now!

There is a win-win situation regarding taxes and retirement. Taking advantage of this strategy allows you to avoid accruing taxes while your money grows, and you are not taxed when your money goes to you. This is the strategy that Mr. Baker used, and it is one that we all should consider.

To find out how this strategy could work for you, go to www.ipadyourmoney.com and schedule a no-obligation conversation with me today.

CHAPTER 4: LIVING BENEFITS – CHRONIC, CRITICAL, & TERMINAL ILLNESS

Timmy's Truck Accident – Part 1

Early in my agency career, on one hot, muggy August afternoon, Julie walked into my office to pay her car insurance. As we completed her transaction, I noticed she only had auto and home insurance.

"Julie, do you have life insurance?" I inquired.

"Yes, I have it through work," she said with a laugh. I can't tell you the number of times that I have gotten that same response from people.

My response to her was, "Well, everyone needs life insurance outside of work." Julie, clearly unamused and with somewhat of a polite snarl on her face, promised to talk it over with her husband, Timmy. I had also heard that numerous times before too.

This time, though, they surprised me. A week and a half later, Julie and Timmy were in my office signing up for life insurance. Timmy was self-employed as a long-distance truck driver who sometimes spent weeks on the road. He didn't have any retirement planning or the typical benefits that an employer would have normally provided. I explained to them that the policy they were getting was more than the typical life insurance policy. It provided cash value and living benefits including critical illness, critical injury, and chronic illness coverage. I further explained that these particular benefits are nice to have "just in case." Little did we know that "just in case" would come in the form of a terrible accident.

Fast forward ten years. I was sitting in my car on a Saturday afternoon in the middle of a thunderstorm, contemplating whether to go home or continue to my destination. My destination was Julie and Timmy's house. For months,

I had been receiving a lot of late payment notices for Julie and Timmy's life insurance premiums. This was highly unusual for them. The phone number I had for them was disconnected and I had not received any correspondence from them. Frankly, I was a bit concerned, but I didn't want to play the role of a bill collector. After discussing it with my wife, I decided to follow my gut and drop by their house. I rang the doorbell, but got no answer. I knocked on the door. Still, no answer. So, I stuck my business card in the screen door with a note to call me. Just as I was heading to my car, their teenage daughter came to the door. I asked her to have her parents call me. She said, "Okay."

Later that evening, Julie called me. I could immediately sense that there was something wrong. Several thoughts began running through my mind. Was she upset that I came by their house? Was she embarrassed? I was not expecting the news that Julie shared next. She said that Timmy had gotten into an accident with his eighteen-wheeler.

Naturally, I asked, "Is he all right?" to which Julie answered, "No, but he is alive."

A few months earlier, while Timmy was driving down the highway, he suffered a medical emergency that resulted in a terrible one-vehicle accident. He spent thirty days on life support at University of Michigan Hospital and was currently in a rehab facility. He was unable to care for himself and would probably never work again.

Julie went on to explain that because Timmy was the primary breadwinner and that she had missed so much work, they were financially devastated on top of everything else.

My next question to her was, "Why didn't you call me?" With a little frustration in her voice, she repeated her earlier statement, "But he's alive. I know we have life insurance, but he survived. There was no reason to call you."

This is why it's so important to have good people on your team, especially when it comes to financial matters and your future. Surely, with everything going on in her life, the last thing that would occur to her is to reach out to me because she was under the illusion that she had no other options when actually, she did. I reminded her of my explanation of the policy's living benefits that she and Timmy signed up for over 10 years prior. "The policy has living benefits!" I told her.

Their policy was not solely a life insurance policy with the common restrictive conditions that many people expect. It covers critical illness, critical injury, and chronic illness. Timmy and Julie made a wise decision in my office, on that day ten years ago. Their choice to cover themselves "just in case" worked well in their favor. We were able to get a claim submitted for Timmy, and today he is collecting those living benefits.

Timmy's accident and medical challenges created a horrible situation. Without the policy they had in place, their circumstances would have likely become worse to the point where they could never recover. Julie and Timmy's situation was somewhat of a rare occurrence, but unexpected incidents happen to people every day.

Occasionally, we also see younger people suffer a heart attack, stroke, or major chronic medical condition that puts them in a similar situation, physically and financially, as it happened to Julie and Timmy. We know all too well that tragedy can befall anyone, regardless of age, race, or economic status. It's best to have some kind of plan in place so that you don't feel like you are out of options, like Julie must have felt before I showed up on her doorstep.

LONG-TERM CARE EXPENSES

As people age, they often find themselves in need of long-term medical care from a home-based or residential medical care facility. The ticket price for this coverage can create quite the burden. The average annual cost of assisted living facilities alone is around $48,000 or higher depending upon the level of care needed. No, your eyes are not fooling you. You read that right. It is a pretty steep ticket and can be even higher depending upon the living arrangements.

The misconception that most people have is that their medical insurance or Medicare will cover any long-term medical costs. I hate to be the bearer of bad news, but, unfortunately, this is far from the truth. My intention is not to villainize these programs, but to shed light on what far too many people fall prey to believing because of a miscommunication or miseducation. Here is the actual language regarding long-term care from the medicare.gov website.

> "Medicare doesn't cover long-term care (also called custodial care) if that's the only care you need. Most nursing home care is custodial care. You pay 100% for non-covered services, including most long-term care.
>
> Long-term care is a range of services and support for your personal care needs. Most long-term care isn't medical care. Instead, most long-term care is to help with basic personal tasks of everyday life like bathing, dressing, and using the bathroom, sometimes called "activities of daily living."

Because long-term care expenses are not covered by health insurance or Medicare, the next obvious place to turn is Medicaid. Medicaid is a federal and state welfare program that helps with healthcare costs for some people with limited income and resources. Medicaid also offers benefits not normally covered by Medicare, including nursing home care and personal care services. This sounds like a viable solution until we consider the eligibility requirements to be covered by Medicaid.

Here are a few of the eligiblity requirements for Medicaid:

Income Limit: If you are single, your income from all sources cannot exceed $16,385 per year, or $1,366 per month. This amount increases to $22,108 per year or $1,842 per month for a married couple. If you are a resident in a nursing home, you are allowed to keep $30-$60 of your monthly income to purchase personal items. The remainder goes to cover your medical costs.

Assets: A single applicant who is 65 or older can possess up to $2,000 in cash, stocks, bonds, certificates of deposit (CDs) and other liquid assets. This includes accounts such as an IRA, 401(k), 403(b) and other tax qualified retirement accounts. It also includes other investments and income property.

Primary home: An applicant's primary residence is exempt if it meets a few fundamental requirements. The home must be in the same state in which the owner is applying for Medicaid, and the applicant must either continue residing in the primary residence or have an "intent and medical ability to return home" as determined by their state.

Car: One automobile of any current market value is considered a "non-countable" asset for Medicaid purposes, as long as it is used for the transportation of the applicant or another member of their household.

As you can see, Medicaid can be a complex issue, and the eligibility requirements can be altogether financially restricting. This is the perfect segue to discuss the spend down process. Spend down is a term used for the process of using all of one's own money and other assets until you have spent enough to qualify for Medicaid.

There are some acceptable spend-down expenses including medical needs, equipment such as eyeglasses, hearing aids, and mobility aids, prepaid funeral expenses, necessary home modifications, and/or a few purchases to make life in a nursing home more comfortable. The key is to avoid penalties that can be assessed. This can be done by not giving or transferring any of your assets to others within the look-back period.

The look back period is normally five years. Basically, the state will "look back" over the recipient's financial records over the last five years to determine how much they have in total assets. Anyone caught in violation during the look back period can be disqualified from receiving Medicaid benefits. As discussed earlier, many individuals rely on Medicaid for critical care and long-term care expenses. It would be grossly unfortunate to be excluded from receiving what you need because you failed to meet the eligbility requirements.

The allowable spend-down expenses combined with the eligibility requirements listed above will determine how much the recipient and their family will have to pay out of pocket before Medicaid will cover any of the long-term medical expenses. There are some variations from state to state in terms of how they will enforce these rules, so it's important to look into your state's specific guidelines. For example, some states will not require the primary home to be sold until after the recipient/patient has passed away. Other states require the home to be sold upfront.

LONG-TERM CARE INSURANCE

A possible solution to avoid the spend down process is to purchase long-term care insurance. It is an insurance policy that helps pay for long-term care expenses. Long-term care insurance covers care generally not covered by ordinary health insurance or Medicare. These policies are typically very comprehensive. The benefits are usually paid in a daily amount, such as $150 per day with an annual or lifetime limit. However, the rising cost of long-term care expenses, which can exceed $225 per day, has caused two problems.

The first issue is that the number of insurance companies that offer long-term care insurance is shrinking almost daily. According to the National Association of Insurance Commissioners, the number of plans offered in the individual and group market through employers has been decreasing over the last 20 years.

The second issue is the expensive cost of obtaining a long term care policy. For example, according to the American Association for Long-Term Care Insurance, a 55-year-old male could expect to pay an annual premium of $2,050 for a policy with a limit of $164,000 in 2019. If that policy included a provision to increase the benefit amount to keep pace with inflation at 3%, the premium would increase to $2,700 per year.

Furthermore, the premium could go up after you buy the policy. Premiums are not guaranteed to stay the same over your lifetime. Additionally, the premium is a "use it or lose it" proposition, just like most other insurances. Take, for instance, the auto insurance you had on your first vehicle. You might have been fortunate enough to not have any accidents with it, but you were still required to pay insurance every month. Did the insurance company refund you for unclaimed funds once the policy was canceled? The answer is no. The same applies with long-term care insurance. In the event that you don't ever use the policy, there is no return of premium, cash value, or death benefit included.

LIFE INSURANCE WITH LIVING BENEFITS

A viable solution for many people is to obtain life insurance that also contains living benefits, which can be used to offset long-term care expenses, critical illness expenses, and critical injury expenses. Oftentimes, this solution is much more affordable but should not be confused with comprehensive long-term care insurance. These are life insurance policies with riders that extend additional coverage to the client which is actually an advancement of the death benefit.

The fact that there is a death benefit means that if the client does not use the living benefits, his or her beneficiary will receive the proceeds from the life policy. Not all life insurance policies with living benefits are created equal. For example, some require a nursing home stay in order to pay the benefits while others do not. Let's take a closer look at two of the recommended living benefits.

CHRONIC ILLNESS

A chronic illness rider is a life insurance option that gives you a way to tap into life insurance benefits while still alive if you are diagnosed with a qualifying chronic illness. This is considered an accelerated death benefit rider and is sometimes added to policies at no extra cost. Chronically ill means that the insured has been certified by a licensed health care practitioner as being unable to perform 2 out of the 6 activities of daily living or is cognitively impaired (i.e., dementia or Alzheimer's). The activities of daily living are bathing, continence, dressing, eating, toileting, and transferring.

CRITICAL ILLNESS AND CRITICAL INJURY

Some insurance companies combine these two riders into one while others list them separately. These riders allow for the payment of a portion of the insured's death benefit if the insured experiences a qualifying medical condition.

The qualifying medical conditions may include aorta graft surgery, aplastic anemia, cancer, cystic fibrosis, diagnosis of ALS, kidney failure, heart attack, heart valve replacement, major organ transplant, motor neuron disease, stroke, sudden cardiac arrest, coma, severe body burns, or traumatic brain injury.

Keep it REAL!

1. Are you prepared for a medical emergency or critical illness?
2. Are you concerned about the spend down process?
3. How would you pay for long-term care or nursing home?

Take Action Now!

> "Action is the foundational key to all success."
> — PABLO PICASSO

We plan for the worst, but hope for the best. Timothy and Julie had no idea what their fate had in store, as none of us do. This is the sentiment of this chapter. Now, it is up to you to take action.

Go to www.ipadappointment.com and schedule your free no obligation consultation today.

CHAPTER 5: YOUR LIFE, YOUR LEGACY

ONE FAMILY'S NIGHTMARE

One fall evening in October, I met with Janice Johnson and her family at their three-bedroom, two-bath, red-brick home outside of Charlotte, NC. Janice was forty-four years old. Her three children, ages eighteen, thirteen, and eleven, joined me at the kitchen table. Curtis, her forty-two-year-old husband, was busy when he walked in, but joined us a bit later in the conversation. They were the picture-perfect middle-class family. A husband and wife working hard to provide for their family. They were good parents and wanted the best for their children.

As the conversation unfolded, I discovered that Curtis didn't have life insurance. I immediately said, "Man, look, you need life insurance, so let's get you taken care of tonight." Although Janice needed and wanted additional life insurance, she did have some coverage through her employer. Curtis became the priority of this first conversation.

I spent the rest of the evening explaining and completing the application for an index universal life policy for Curtis. He was a slender guy, standing almost six feet tall. From his size, I'd say he was about 180 pounds and the picture of good health. It took about a week to get his policy approved, which is standard for someone without any health concerns.

A few weeks later, I delivered the policy and went over the details with Janice and Curtis. I remember it vividly. He thanked me, gave me a fist bump, and then ran out to take his son to the barbershop. I stayed with Janice and their other two children to complete a life insurance application for her.

About a month and a half later, I was in Birmingham doing my last conference of the year before taking a break for Christmas. My phone buzzed in my pocket. I reached down and squeezed the button to send the caller to voicemail. Just as I raised my hand out my pocket, it buzzed again. This happened two more times before the buzzing finally stopped.

When my presentation transitioned to the Q&A, I looked at my phone and saw three missed calls from Janice. I also had an unread text message but had been unable to look at it right away. When the questions concluded, I finished my presentation, shook a few hands, booked a few appointments, and packed my things. While heading to my car to return to the hotel for the evening, I called Janice.

Janice answered the phone quickly; immediately I knew something was wrong. From the tone of her voice, I could tell she had been crying. She tearfully spoke into the phone. "Curtis was killed in a car accident!" Shocked by the news, I sat and prayed silently, listening for what else she wanted to share. She went on to say, "He got hit by three cars. He got hit by three cars!"

She continued on to explain what happened. It was a rainy morning when Curtis left home and caught the train to work. When he got off the train to cross the street, he was struck by a car. The impact of the car knocked him into oncoming traffic, and he was hit by a second car. Then, he was run over while lying in the road by a third car. He died at the scene of the accident.

Curtis' death was tragic and unimaginable. Of course, I could not undo what happened, but I am thankful for the brief presence that I had in their lives. I felt a solemn sense of peace, knowing that I served their family well by making sure that when I left after that first meeting, Curtis had life insurance.

As any loving wife would, Janice spoke about the payment she had received from the life policy, saying she would rather have her husband than the money. However, the life insurance proceeds allowed her to maintain her current standard of living and create a family legacy in honor of Curtis.

ARE YOU PREPARED?

A man that has not prepared his children for his own death has failed as a father.
— T'CHAKA TO T'CHALLA, THE BLACK PANTHER MOVIE

Fortunately, tragedies like that of Curtis Johnson do not happen in our lives very often. However, it is far too common to see people die with little to no life insurance. Perhaps you have seen or even given to a Go-Fund-Me campaign to cover the funeral costs of someone who died without life insurance. Because life (and death) happens unexpectedly, not being prepared is simply not acceptable.

The lack of life insurance is a critical problem that transcends age, gender, and race. Not having life insurance is far more costly than believing we are invincible until we reach our golden years. It is not typical for college-age students to consider buying life insurance. Similarly, health-conscious individuals may think their fit lifestyles will keep them going and going for years to come. While I do not want to discount the significance of time and health, unforeseen tragedies can befall anyone at any time.

According to Policygenius in a 2021 survey, only 54% of adults have any type of life insurance. Half this number only have it through their employers, which is not enough. In Chapter three, I shared that fifty million people lost their jobs due to COVID-19. Here is how these statistics apply to that particular sub-group of the U.S. population:

- 23 million people had no life insurance when the pandemic started.
- An additional 11 million lost their life insurance during the pandemic.
- 14 million of 50 million remain with life insurance…a mere 28%

At the time of drafting this book, there were over 600,000 COVID-19 related deaths in the United States. With a statistical insured rate of only 28%, there have been an estimated 432,000+ COVID-19 related deaths, with no life insurance in force. To put this number in perspective, that would be the equivalent of the entire population of cities like, Miami, FL; Oakland, CA; Tulsa, OK; Minnesota, MN, and Raleigh, NC…just to name a few.

Now, here is a question to ponder: "Did we really need a global pandemic to make us realize the need to take care of this very basic, fundamental, financial responsibility?" Yes, it is a financial responsibility. If you truly care for the people in your life, such as your spouse, your children, your grandchildren, and your parents, you will make sure to get the proper life insurance today.

Why? It is not about "if" we will die someday, but "when". When the inevitable occurs, will your passing create more pain to your loved ones because of the burden of funeral expenses and the loss of income to provide their living expenses? Whether you are the primary breadwinner of the home or not, those we leave behind will bear some financial hardship from our death. Being proactive in creating a cushion is a considerable gesture of love.

There was one particular instance when my wife and I were out shopping. A gentleman came up to me and asked if I was Tony Jackson. I replied, "Yes." Next, the gentleman told me that I had saved his family. Of course, I was curious. How often do you hear a statement like when you meet a stranger? I asked him to explain.

He went on to tell me that he listened to me on Facebook Live, discuss the importance of life insurance. He showed me a text message, where he urged his sister to get life insurance based on what he learned from me. His sister took action and bought a life insurance policy. Six months later, she died unexpectedly. The life insurance proceeds allowed his family to take care of her final expenses, among other things.

I am urging you to take action today. Schedule your free no obligation conversation with me at www.ipadappointment.com.

HOW MUCH LIFE INSURANCE IS ENOUGH?

I know Black Lives Matter, but how much is a black life worth?

— EUGENE MITCHELL, AUTHOR OF CLOSING THE RACIAL WEALTH GAP

So, how much life insurance is enough? I am often presented with this question for which there is no definitive answer. The short answer is that it depends. A vast number of worksheets and financial calculators are available to produce a magical answer to the question, but everyone is different. Therefore, everyone's needs are different as well. I will share a simple approach to determine your basic life insurance needs.

Before discussing how to arrive at the "number," it is important to have the appropriate mindset. The need for life insurance goes far beyond the money needed to cover the cost of a funeral. Here is a partial list of things to consider.

- **Loans and Debt:** How much will be needed upon your death to pay your loans and debts, i.e. mortgage, student loans, automobile loans, and credit card debt?

You might be surprised how many people think that debt goes away when someone dies, but this cannot be further from the truth. It would be nice if everything got wiped away at death, but it just does not work that way. What happens is that debt often gets passed onto the loved ones left behind. Student loans fortunately can be canceled when someone dies if there is no cosigner or if it's not a parent plus loan. Other outstanding debts, however, must be satisfied, and creditors will do all they can to get repayment.

- **Income Replacement:** How much of your annual income will your spouse and/or family need if you were to die today? How long will they need it? When considering income replacement, think about the dollar amount you make before taxes and other deductions, also called gross income. Often, when calculating income replacement needs, people use their net income, but so much happens between total wages and the income you bring home that doing so will not produce an accurate number. Also, consider the age of your loved ones. For example, if you have young children, you will want to factor in the expenses needed to maintain the household you are leaving behind and education costs up to adult age.

- **Final Expenses:** What is the cost of a funeral? Other final expenses include death taxes on retirement accounts, attorney and court fees, and expenses ·related to the transfer of property and other financial assets. The reason funerals are notorious for dividing families is because most people have no idea how expensive funerals are; this ignorance causes a boatload of extra grief. Many families cannot properly grieve the loss of their loved one because they are dealing with financial anxiety. There are costs for storing and preparing the body, the funeral staff, a plot burial or cremation processing, all of which are costs that no one wants to think about until the time comes. The charges are unexpectedly hefty and blindsiding.

- **Extra Things:** Extra things include setting up an emergency fund for the family left behind, establishing an educational fund for the children or grandchildren, creating a family legacy or trust, etc. Life is full of extra things you need to be prepared for. Fortunately, if you think big picture or long term, you can realistically factor in the necessary life expenditures. In comparison to past generations, people today are living under the best conditions and health, and with more opportunities than ever seen before. This means that people are branching out from a survival-only means of living and thinking longer-term, sustainable living. More parents are considering trust funds for their children or creating college funds to ease the financial burden for education in later years. Likewise, we are in an overall better condition to ease our spouse's transition if we pass away, by considering the type of lifestyle they deserve in our absence.

Once you have considered and determined the amount needed for these four areas, the formula is simple. Use the acronym L.I.F.E. (Loans + Income Replacement + Final Expenses + Extras = Life Insurance Need). For those who prefer a complicated formula, we can take into consideration things like the time value of money, inflation, expected investment returns, etc.

If you are a person who likes to err on the side of caution, you may feel more comfortable overcompensating, so you are sure to cover everything. While it may be arguable, I doubt it is possible to be over prepared. Especially when it comes to inflation. Who knows what the dollar will be worth in the next fifty years?

I discussed the time value of money earlier in this book. If invested wisely, your dollar today can multiply its value. This should be another incentive to get started today.

IT'S MORE THAN A DEATH BENEFIT

I don't call it "Life Insurance," I call it "Love Insurance." We buy it because we want to leave a legacy for those we love.

— FARSHAD ASL

Let's be honest, there is a stigma when it comes to life insurance. I have often joked that I lost half my friends when I became a life insurance agent. (By the way, I lost the other half when I became a preacher).

There is a long list of previously held ideas that need restructuring, but for the sake of brevity and sticking to the point, the message here will focus on life insurance. Why are some people afraid to get life insurance? Yes, inquiring about life insurance really does put fear in people's minds. Some avoid it because it seems too heavy or insignificant in their world. Does inquiring about how to protect yourself and your loved ones suddenly change the fate of your life? Honestly, more people should be apprehensive about *not* having life insurance.

I have heard every excuse in the book from "I don't want to jinx myself" and "I don't care what happens after I am gone" to "I don't want to make somebody else rich when I die" and "I can't afford it." The list of excuses goes on and on. We love to toss around words like "legacy" or "generational wealth." Well, life insurance is the most practical and economic way to create both a legacy and generational wealth. Here's a direct quote from Investopedia:

> *One result of accumulating wealth may be the desire to keep it in the family by passing along assets to future generations. Life Insurance is a popular way for the wealthy to maximize their after-tax estate and have more money to pass on to heirs. A life insurance policy can be used as an investment tool or simply provide added financial reassurance. While life insurance isn't something wealthy people alone can benefit from, there are several unique reasons someone may consider purchasing it.*

Here is a list of some of the unique attributes of life insurance:

- tax laws favor life insurance
- life insurance can protect business owners
- life insurance is an Class A asset
- life insurance is a retirement strategy
- life insurance doesn't discriminate against race or gender
- life insurance can close wealth gaps
- life insurance can fit into your budget

LEGENDS AND LIFE INSURANCE

Due to the reasons outlined above, people like Mr. Baker and countless others have taken advantage of having life insurance as part of their overall financial portfolio. Next we look at three legendary businessmen who utilized life insurance to create tremendous financial legacies.

JC Penney. During the great depression, JC Penney stores and the chain owner, James Cash Penney, experienced tremendous losses in his business and personal finances. However, Mr. Penney had accumulated a tremendous amount of cash value inside of his life insurance policies. He used this cash value to keep his stores afloat and eventually transformed the chain into a national retail giant. The following excerpt is from a 1971 New York Times article about John Cash Penney at the time of his death.

In 1922 he insured himself for $3-million, one of the largest life insurance policies issued up to that time. Then disaster struck. The 1929 stock market crash sent Penney stock plunging from 120 points to 13, and Mr. Penney lost $40 million dollars. Starting anew with money borrowed on his life insurance, he regained a foothold in the company...the Penney chain became the country's fifth largest merchandising company, with sales of $4.1 billion.

McDonald's. The fast-food chain we often refer to as "the golden arches" is owned by Ray Kroc. At its onset, McDonalds was a partnership between Mr. Kroc and two brothers, Richard and Maurice McDonald. In 1961, after six years, the McDonald's system had been developed; Mr. Kroc bought out the McDonald brothers and became the sole owner for 2.7 million dollars. The acquisition was very difficult and left Mr. Kroc strapped for money. However, he used the cash value from his two life insurance policies to personally survive, pay his key employees, and launch a mascot known as Ronald McDonald. Today, McDonald's is arguably the most recognized fast-food chain in the world.

The Walt Disney Corporation. Disney is a mass media and entertainment conglomerate that transcends the global space as a financial powerhouse. This was not the case in the post-World War II years during which Disney was struggling to make a profit. Walt Disney had a dream of revitalizing his company with the opening of an amusement park. Mr. Disney went to several banks to get funding for his amusement park but was turned down by each of them. Since no banker would loan him the money, Disney borrowed from his life insurance policy to fund Disneyland. The following is a direct quote from Walt Disney, himself...

> *It takes a lot of money to make dreams come true. From the very start it was a problem. Getting the money to open Disneyland... And we had everything mortgaged, including my personal insurance...*

Your Legacy. The bottom line is that we are all creating a legacy. It's either a positive legacy or a legacy that is not quite complete. In either case, it will have an impact for generations. The decision whether or not to purchase life insurance as part of your legacy is your choice. We each make a choice to either purchase life insurance or roll the dice without it. When making that choice, weigh all life insurance options, consider your primary reasons for purchasing coverage, and how much money your beneficiaries will need when you die.

Keep it REAL!

1. How long could your family survive without your income?
2. Do you have enough life insurance?
3. Does your life insurance policy provide tax-free cash value?

Take Action Now!

Choose wisely…schedule your appointment today at www.ipadappointment.com

CHAPTER 6: PROTECT YOUR LEGACY...LEGALLY

TIMMY'S TRUCK ACCIDENT - PART TWO

Let's take a moment and revisit the story of Julie and Timmy, the truck driver from Chapter four. As you recall, Julie and Timmy purchased an indexed universal life policy that included the living benefits of critical and chronic illness. Despite the unfortunate tragedy, I am sure that

Julie and Timmy share my sentiment of being truly thankful that they selected a policy that included this coverage.

However, there was a challenge when it came to processing Timmy's claim. Julie was listed as the primary beneficiary on Timmy's policy. Therefore, upon his death, Julie would have complete control over the policy benefits. Fortunately, Timmy did not die in the truck accident. Julie still had her husband, and their children hadn't lost their father. Therefore, as the owner of the policy, he remained in control. Although I formally filed his claim, he needed to make the final decisions regarding the acceptance and payment of those benefits.

The problem is that Timmy was not mentally or physically able to make those decisions. Furthermore, Julie and Timmy did not have a will, financial power of attorney, or health care power of attorney in place. Suppose they had those basic estate planning documents in place. Julie could have stepped in with no issues and made all of the necessary decisions regarding the policy benefits. Without either in place, however, Julie had to petition the court system to obtain the appropriate authorization. This process caused unnecessary delays in getting the benefits started.

LEGENDS AND LEGAL LEGACY

Far too many entertainment legends have died unexpectedly without the basic estate planning documents formally in place. For the sake of brevity, let's have a look at a few of the big names.

- **James Brown.** The Godfather of soul died on Christmas Day of 2006. Without the proper will, or more importantly, a trust in place, a three-year battle ensued over his estate. To settle the bitter dispute, a South Carolina judge ordered that 50% of the Brown estate go to charity. The lower court's decision was challenged, and a final settlement was decided by the South Carolina Supreme Court nearly fourteen years after his death.

- **Prince.** One of the greatest and best-selling musical artists of all time died in 2016 without a will. As of the writing of this book, his estate still has not been settled. His estate is allegedly worth over 100 million dollars and has been placed in the hands of a Minnesota probate court. The true value of his estate, the identity of his siblings, and how the estate will be distributed will be determined by the court.

- **Aretha Franklin.** The Queen of Soul died in August of 2016. Reportedly, she had a handwritten will; however, her family was not able to locate it. Had it been found, her estate would have undoubtedly still landed in probate court. Informal estate documents are not legally binding.

Contrary to the cases of the mega stars above, the story of Michael Jackson is completely different. The King of Pop died unexpectedly on June 25, 2009. Michael was one of the most successful entertainers of all time, and his estate was said to be worth more than 1.3 billion dollars according to the IRS. Michael had established a trust in 1995 and later updated it to the Michael Jackson Family Trust in 2002 to protect and preserve his estate for his children and his mother.

The IRS did come after his estate, and his 21-page trust document prevailed in court. He had a last will and testament - only a five-page document designed to catch all the assets that might have been missed by the trust. Ultimately these 26 pages of estate plan documents ensured that his mother and children would benefit from his enormous estate with minimum tax implications.

As you can see, there is a clear distinction between the outcome for going that extra mile to spell out the details and the failure to do so. Of course, there is nothing wrong with donating your hard-earned money to charity. I am sure the charities that receive funds from estates are very grateful. All the same, I am willing to bet that you would prefer to decide how your money is spent and to whom it goes. Leaving these matters to a legal entity means that a stranger will determine the best course of action. More commonly, not having an estate plan results in tremendous legal fees and taxes which ultimately results in no legacy, charitable gift, etc.

PROBATE COURT

Investopedia defines probate court as *"a segment of the judicial system that primarily handles such matters as wills, estates, conservatorships, and guardianships."* When wills are contested, for example, the probate court is responsible for ruling on the authenticity of the document and the mental stability of the person who signed it. The court also decides who receives which portion of the deceased's assets, based on the instructions in the will.

When there is no will or estate planning measure in place, such as a trust, the probate court must determine who is the next of kin and what portion of the deceased's estate each individual receives. The average time it takes to go through probate nationally is nine months, but as indicated above, in some cases it can last for years. Sometimes the person designated to act as the representative of the estate, also called the executor, does not want to be involved. In some cases, family members are estranged from one another, and communication is a challenge. There may be holes in the estate plan that must be worked out first.

In addition to the time involved, the process can also be very expensive. Attorney fees can range between $250 to $300 per hour. Some attorneys will charge a flat fee of around 30% of the estate's value, depending upon the complexity of the case.

WHO SHOULD HAVE AN ESTATE PLAN?

Estate planning is an important and everlasting gift you can give your family. And setting up a smooth inheritance isn't as hard as you might think.

— SUSIE ORMAN

It is time to put to rest the misguided thought that estate planning is only for the rich and wealthy. My client, Timmy, although not rich or wealthy, certainly could have benefited from proper estate planning. Anyone who has assets and wants to pass them on to their survivors such as a spouse or children should have an estate plan. Anyone means everyone: single, married, young, old, male, female, rich or poor.

Additionally, I want to specifically address one group: parents. It is my belief that most parents want to ensure that their children are properly cared for in the event of their death or incapacity. For estate planning purposes, assets would include property, personal belongings, bank accounts, stocks, mutual funds, retirement accounts, and life insurance - just to create a partial list.

The key is to minimize the probate court process along with court fees, attorney fees, and delays. Probate court can be a lengthy, stressful process. The more things you have spelled out, the easier the proceedings will go, and no detail is too small.

WHAT SHOULD BE INCLUDED IN AN ESTATE PLAN

Estate plans can be very complex, depending upon the number and amount of assets involved, combined with the dynamics of the family structure. Outlined below are some of the basic documents that should be found in every estate plan.

Last Will & Testament. A will or testament is a legal document that expresses a person's wishes of how their property is to be distributed after their death. It also names the guardian's and other family's desires when minor children are involved. It is important to note that a will does not necessarily avoid probate court, but it does direct the court about how the deceased wanted their assets managed.

Durable Power of Attorney (POA). A POA gives an individual or organization the authority to conduct financial and business transactions in the event of his/her death or inability to act on their own behalf. Without a POA, the court will appoint and authorize someone to carry out the legal and financial decisions for the deceased. This may result in their wishes and desires not going as planned.

Healthcare Power of Attorney (HCPA). This document designates another individual (typically a spouse or family member) to make important healthcare decisions on your behalf in the event of incapacity. This person should be someone you trust who shares your values and religious beliefs.

Healthcare Directive. This document is very closely related to the HCPA. They both protect your rights as they relate to healthcare issues and health insurance policies to ensure you get the care you desire. A Healthcare Directive dictates what medical care you want to receive (i.e., life support, etc.). and the HCPA gives the individual the authority to carry out the directive.

OWN NOTHING, BUT CONTROL EVERYTHING

"Own nothing but control everything" is the tagline that many financial professionals use when discussing a trust. What is meant here is that one of the primary purposes of a trust is ownership of all your assets while you maintain control of the trust. The basic definition of trust is a legal vehicle that allows a third party, a trustee, to hold and direct assets in a trust fund on behalf of the beneficiary.

A trust greatly expands your options when it comes to managing assets, whether you're trying to shield your wealth from taxes or pass it on to your children. A trust can be a great strategy to avoid the spend down process that is explained in chapter 4. If you don't legally own any assets, then you have no assets to spend down in order to get Medicaid to cover your long-term medical expenses.

Here are the primary parties of a trust.

- **Grantor of the Trust.** The person who creates a trust and transfers property to it is called the *grantor*. A grantor is sometimes called a *settlor*, *maker*, *donor* or *trustor*. In a living trust, the grantor retains the right to amend, alter or revoke the trust.

- **Trustee and Successor Trustee.** The person in charge of managing the trust, often the same person who created the trust, is called a *trustee*. In most states, any person or entity (such as banks, trust companies and some brokerage firms) capable of taking legal title to the property can be appointed trustee. Trustees have a legal duty (often called a *fiduciary duty*) to protect the assets of the trust and ensure that the purposes of the trust are followed.

- **Beneficiaries.** The person who benefits from the trust is the *beneficiary*. The beneficiary is entitled to receive the benefits of the income and principal of the trust. There are several categories: the primary beneficiary, the contingent beneficiary (sometimes referred to as a secondary beneficiary), and the remainder beneficiary.

In terms of the trusts themselves, there are several kinds. Each type has its primary purpose. Here are the two most common types of trusts.

- **Revocable Trust.** A revocable trust, such as a living trust, is used to avoid having the estate go through probate court. The term "revocable" means that assets can be removed from the control of the trust. As indicated in the cases outlined earlier, probate can be lengthy, expensive and often brutal. Your heirs can become emotionally and financially exhausted when going through this process. Think of setting up a trust as an extension of the love you want to leave behind. You can prevent a tremendous amount of stress.

- **Irrevocable Trust.** Opposite to revocable trusts, assets in an irrevocable trust cannot be removed or amended after they've been placed in the trust. Since total control of assets have been relinquished, they are effective in protecting your assets from possible estate taxes and the spend down process. It also avoids probate court.

PROTECTING GENERATIONAL WEALTH

Proper estate planning is often overlooked in the conversation involving generational wealth. We would much rather focus on how to accumulate wealth and simply ignore that we all are going to eventually pass away. The reality is that after someone dies, the grief of their loss can be a challenging time for the remaining family, friends, and loved ones. Emotionally, it can cut deep. Without life insurance, it can also be a tremendous financial burden.

Unfortunately, the probate court process can add an additional financial challenge and pain. If someone is not properly prepared, it can wipe out all of one's accumulated wealth. This can easily result in a perpetual "starting at the bottom" financial situation for the future generations of the family.

Having a proper estate plan in place can preserve generational wealth for every branch that blossoms from your family tree. Instead of starting from scratch, family members can build from a wise decision to plan well and think ahead.

Keep it REAL!

1. Do you have a will or trust?
2. If so, when was it last updated?
3. Does it include a Financial Power of Attorney, Healthcare Power of Attorney, and a Medical Directive?

As you can see, estate planning, especially advanced instruments such as trusts, can be a very complex issue. Legal council should be consulted. You will want to consider the assets in your estate that you will leave behind and how they can best benefit your loved ones. Take action to put the proper estate plans in place.

For more information, visit www.trmclegalshield.com and schedule a conversation at www.ipadappointment.com.

CHAPTER 7 - PULLING IT ALL TOGETHER... STEP BY STEP

It's not about how much money you make, it's about how much you keep.

— JOHN LYNCH

Over the last six chapters, I have presented you with a lot of financial and technical information. For many readers, this may have been the first time you have been exposed to some of these concepts and strategies. Hopefully, I did not lose you in any investment or money jargon, but rather you were able to grasp the meat and potatoes of this entire book. The end goal is for you to make better money decisions.

In an effort to bring clarity and understanding, I have begun each chapter with an example or story. Although the names and places have been changed, these are true stories with real clients. The most compelling of these stories is the contrast of Mrs. Jones and Mr. Baker from Chapter Three. The contrast between these two wonderful clients exposes the difference of following the "traditional" money rules such as 401(k), 403(b), TSP, etc. versus playing by the "smart" money rules that utilize other strategies such as cash value life insurance. To pull it all together in a hypothetical life scenario, let's take one last look at Mrs. Jones' and Mr. Baker's financial journey.

MRS. JONES' CONTRIBUTIONS

Now, remember Mrs. Jones was a teacher. She did everything right. She implemented the traditional money rules playbook exactly as we have been taught to do. She got a good education and a good job with benefits and a retirement plan. She contributed $5,000 per year into the school district's optional 403(b) retirement plan in addition to her mandatory contributions into the state pension plan.

As time went by, Mrs. Jones, from time to time, expressed some concern and anxiety about the fluctuations in the stock market. Her portfolio performed well over many years but market volatility in recent years was becoming more concerning especially as a retiree in her golden years. To cover her family's life insurance needs, she purchased a $500,000 30-year term policy at the age 40. This policy cost her about $1,000 each year but had now expired with no cash value or return of the $30,000 of premiums she paid.

MR. BAKER'S CONTRIBUTIONS

Now, Mr. Baker was an independent contractor. Therefore, he had no employer retirement plan such as a 401(k), nor did he have any type of employer match. However, he contributed about $6,000 per year into a cash value life insurance policy. His death benefit for this policy started at $500,000 but grew over time. Mr. Barker did not like to "play" the stock market. It was very comforting for him to know that he never lost any money due to market fluctuations. This is the very policy that afforded him the ability to withdraw $50,000 to buy the brand new Cadillac Escalade with no stress, no debt, and no taxes.

MRS. JONES' ESTATE PLAN

Although Mrs. Jones recognized the importance of having a will, she was not exposed to the true value of a comprehensive estate plan. Therefore, she found herself having the need to establish a trust much later in life. Fortunately for her, she never experienced the need for nursing home care. However, she worried about losing her assets during the spend down process if her health deteriorated to the point that she would needed long term care.

MR. BAKER'S ESTATE PLAN

Mr. Baker bought a family legal plan which was used to complete his Will, Power of Attorney and Health Care Power of Attorney. As time went on, he accumulated a substantial amount of assets. He also formed a living trust to ensure that his beneficiaries would receive the generational wealth that he worked so hard to establish. This gave him a peace of mind as he continued to age and deal with some serious health challenges.

MRS. JONES' LIFE AFTER RETIREMENT

To be very honest, Mrs. Jones is enjoying a comfortable retirement. Like many retirees, one of her main concerns is running out of money during her lifetime. Her 403(b)-retirement plan comes with no lifetime income guarantees. In addition, let me remind you of her major question to me in chapter 3… "Why am I paying so much in taxes?"

Here is the reality. If she wants $3000 per month out of her 403(b), she has to withdraw $4000 because at least $1,000 will be paid in taxes. At that rate, her 403(b) money could run out in around 11 years. Once this happens, she will be living off of her state pension and Social Security only.

The industry standard for years is that you should not withdraw over 4% of your total account value each year in order for you not to run out of money during your retirement years. Under the current conditions, *Yahoo! Money* suggests that a withdrawal rate of 3-3.5% is more appropriate. In either case, Mrs. Jones would need a total retirement of nearly $1.5 million dollars in order to withdraw $4,000 per month and have a reasonable expectation that her income would not run out during retirement.

MR. BAKER'S LIFE AFTER RETIREMENT

Mr. Baker also enjoys a comfortable retirement. However, he has had the financial freedom to travel quite a bit more in that new Cadillac Escalade. He spends most of the winter months traveling throughout the warmer states pulling his RV. He and his wife particularly enjoy the campgrounds in the Southwestern states like Arizona and Nevada, while still maintaining their home in Michigan. The thing that has made such a difference for Mr. Baker is that he is getting a lifetime, tax-free income of $38,000 per year from his cash value life insurance to supplement his social security and other retirement income.

Yes, it is both a guaranteed lifetime benefit and it's income tax-free! Therefore, marketing fluctuations are of no concern for him. Income taxes are of no concern for him. As he approaches 90 years old, he has pulled out over $800,000 in income and paid zero taxes.

MRS. JONES' LEGACY

Mrs. Jones' legacy is certainly moving in a great direction. She has been fortunate as it relates to her health. She has remained very active and has a great workout regimen, even though she is well into her 70's. I was able to rollover some of her retirement funds into a fixed indexed annuity to protect those funds from a market crash when the next one occurs. It also provides lifetime income benefits even if her other retirement funds run out of money. Equally as important, I was able to put her into an index universal life policy that provides her with chronic and critical illness benefits if the need arises. The death benefit will provide additional funds to her family to cover the tax burden that occurs when they inherit her unused retirement funds.

When I began working with Mrs. Jones, she had very little debt. I was able to create a plan for her to become totally debt free. Today, she has no debt, including no mortgage. The bottom line here is that it's never too late. Mrs. Jones immediately put many of the principles that I have written about into action. She didn't say "It's too late for me" or "I'm too old." She also understands that had she known about these principles earlier in life, it would have been much less expensive to implement and the impact would be much greater in establishing generational wealth.

MR. BAKER'S LEGACY

The trajectory of Mr. Baker's legacy was set well before I met him. I was just fortunate enough to witness it and help him carry it out. Unfortunately, Mr. Baker has had some serious health challenges and now requires long-term care. He has been able to receive this care at his home in Michigan. His life insurance policy covers most of the cost of having a CNA (certified nurse assistant) visit him daily.

Mr. Baker's assets are held inside of a trust. Therefore, if he does get to the point that he needs to be admitted into a nursing home, he will not have any issues having Medicaid pay any shortfall as relates to the cost. Upon his eventual death, his assets including property will easily transfer to his beneficiaries. In addition, Mr. Baker has over $500,000 of life insurance benefits that will also be tax-free to his beneficiaries. Generations of his family will benefit from the decisions he made early in life.

MY CONCLUDING THOUGHTS

Lots of people go through their entire life and, at the end of it, never find answers to the questions they've always wondered about. Or the reasons they stayed where they are, doing the same things day after day, week after week and year after year, always wondering why their lives never seemed to change.

— ROBERT WOLFF

One of our greatest assets in life and one that we probably do not appreciate until we are older, is time. In this business, I've met with many people. It's not uncommon for a young person to think, "I'm young. I don't need to worry about this right now. I'll just save money myself. I have time." Ah, but do you?

One thing about life that I have come to know and respect is the value of time. Yes, I talk about the value of time as it pertains to money, but time plays such an important role in the decisions we make as well. Of course, a young person is more likely to be less concerned about retirement than someone nearing retirement age. Still, time neither stops nor waits for anyone. The saying that pops into my mind right now is, "Don't put off until tomorrow what you can do today." Tomorrow will come sooner than you think.

Many of us have heard, or even said, "If I knew then what I know now!" This statement holds true for many aspects of life including our handling, investing, and protecting of our money. As you have read this book, you undoubtedly at some point may have said to yourself "I didn't know that." Well, now you do know. Not only do you know but you have seen the comparison of two very different approaches to wealth and retirement. One by Mrs. Jones and the other by Mr. Baker.

Does your path align closer to Mrs. Jones, Mr. Baker, or neither? They both have been successful in their respective careers and both have prepared well for retirement. Mrs. Jones is a delightful lady and is living life pretty much on her own terms. She is blessed!

Yes, it's true that there are some things that Mr. Baker either knew or stumbled upon that made a difference in his life. You have now been exposed to many of those same things. The imposing question that now remains to be answered is: What are you going to do with this new information? The commonality between Mrs. Jones and Mr. Baker is that both acted upon the information when they got it. They just happened to get it at different stages in life.

There really is no reason to beat yourself up about what you did not know before. Too often we spend too much time deliberating over the past when all we really have is now. The biggest takeaway is to start where you are right now and do better going forward. So, regardless of what stage of life you are in, when this book gets into your hands, you should take action. Now!

At the end of each of the previous six chapters, I have asked a few Keeping It Real questions. My final call to action for you is to go to www.ipadquestions.com and confidentially submit your answers to these self-discovery questions.

1. Where did you learn about money management?
2. Who are your money mentors/influencers?
3. Do you have a budget and/or debt elimination plan?
4. What is your investment risk tolerance: high risk, moderate, or conservative?
5. Have you ever lost money due to stock market declines?
6. Are you concerned about the impact of future market crashes on your money?
7. Are you concerned about the impact of taxes on your retirement funds?
8. Do you have money in all three buckets: taxable, tax deferred, and tax free?
9. Do you have a long-term tax free retirement strategy?
10. Are you prepared for a medical emergency or critical illness?
11. Are you concerned about the spend down process?
12. How would you pay for long-term care or a nursing home care?

13. How long could your family survive without your income?
14. Do you have enough life insurance?
15. Does your life insurance provide tax-free cash value?
16. Do you have a will or trust?
17. If so, when was it updated the last time?
18. Does it include the Financial Power of Attorney, Healthcare Power of Attorney, and a Medical Directive?
19. Do you more closely align with Mrs. Jones or Mr. Baker?
20. Are you ready to take action?

BONUS: THREE THINGS YOU SHOULD KNOW

EVERYTHING YOU JUST LEARNED ACCELERATED

You can leverage your way to a better retirement.
— DANIEL FISHER, FORBES.COM

Michael was from Bowie, Maryland. He was a high school basketball star who won multiple state championships. He was only 5'8" but as the starting point guard, he averaged 21 points and 7 assists per game. He was a scholar, athlete, and a respectable, bright-eyed happy-go-lucky young man. He was raised by a single mother, who put herself through college and worked in the banking industry.

Michael was offered several basketball scholarships. He accepted an offer from a Division 2 college on the east coast. Like many young men in his position, his dream was to play in the NBA. However, he was undersized and played in a league that didn't get him much NBA attention. Even with an outstanding sophomore year, he began to realize that his dream of playing in the NBA was at best a long shot. This was a hard reality for a twenty-year-old young man to accept, especially because he had always been the best player on every team he played on.

While dealing with the emotions of watching his professional dreams become out of reach, his father passed away before his senior year. This impacted his play on the court and his grades off the court. However, Michael inherited nearly $200,000 from his dad.

He and his mother looked for investment opportunities. They had certain criteria:

1. The investment had to be safe so the money wouldn't be lost and
2. The investment had to create a legacy that would live multiple generations.

They decided to invest half of his inheritance in a premium financed indexed universal life policy. When Michael turns 65 years old, the policy is projected to generate over $211,000 of annual tax free income for the rest of his life.

Here's how the plan works.

1. During the first five years, Michael will contribute a total of $97,500 which will be matched by the bank with an additional $63,770
2. In years 6 through 10, the bank will contribute another $153,770
3. Michael contributes 30% of the premium and the other 70% is OPM (Other Peoples Money) from the bank with no promissory note, credit check, or personal guarantees
4. The indexed universal life gives him a death benefit of $1,000,000
5. He also receives terminal, chronic, and critical illness coverages and a projected lifetime annual income of $225,000 tax-free

In essence, he gets everything I wrote about in this book but through a tremendously accelerated program. See the chart below.

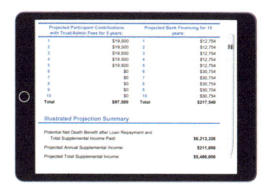

If Mr. Baker had known about this strategy when he started his indexed universal life policy, his results would have been even greater. For example, his total contributions would have dropped from $180,000 over 30 years to $125,000 over 5 years. His initial death benefit would have started at $891,000 rather than $500,000. His annual retirement income would have increased from $38,000, starting at age 67, to over $62,000 per year at age 65. The total tax-free income received would have increased from nearly $800,000 to over $1,600,000.

Obviously, premium financed indexed universal life is not for everyone; however, if you are looking for a retirement plan that allows you to use leveraged money and complete your contributions in just 5 years, it may be the right plan for you. Many people from young athletes to senior executives are taking advantage of one of the most dynamic and innovative retirement programs available on today's market.

To learn more about a premium financed indexed universal life, go to www.TonyJacksonkaiZen.com.

MY MILLION DOLLAR BABY

25% of U.S. households are contributing less toward their children's college education or have stopped saving entirely.
— EDUCATION NEW MAGAZINE

Ben and Sue were high school sweethearts; they were a perfect couple. He was the starting quarterback, and she was captain of the cheerleading squad. Homecoming King and Queen. They went to the same college and eventually got married. They enjoyed a couple of years of married life before starting a family. Their first daughter, Samantha, was a beautiful little girl and their pride and joy. And like many parents, once we have children, we start to think about their future; we start to think about how we could provide for them.

The first major expense that comes to our mind is college. Ben and Sue wanted to make sure that they set Samantha up for a great college experience. They didn't want her to come out of school with a lot of debt. So they began doing what many people do. They started a 529 college savings plan. By the time she was a senior in high school, they had managed to save over $25,000 for Samantha's college education.

Back in those days, $25,000 was a major chunk of her expected college budget. Samantha was also a student-athlete. She was a gifted volleyball player and received a scholarship to play the sport at a small Midwest college. To their surprise, the college financial aid officer informed them that the value of the 529 plan would be subtracted from the athlete scholarship amount. To make matters worse, although the funds they withdrew for Samantha's qualified education expenses were nontaxable, they were considered income to Samantha for financial aid purposes. They were indeed shocked.

Fast forward ten years, Samantha is now married herself and has her first child. Remembering her collegiate experience, she informed her husband, Dan Sr., that she would like to look for an alternative way to save for college other than a 529 plan. In her research she read an article entitled, "Whole Life Insurance vs 529 College Savings Plans."

Ultimately, Samantha and Dan chose to start an indexed universal life program for their son, Dan, Jr. We call the concept My Million Dollar Baby, and here's how it works. The indexed universal life policy has all the same features and benefits outlined in the earlier chapters. These benefits and features include a death benefit, chronic illness, critical illness, and tax-free growth based on a stock market index with no risk of market loss. However, the cash value when withdrawn is not taxed and also not considered for financial aid purposes. Therefore, it does not have any impact on scholarship awards or other financial assistance programs, etc.

Furthermore, if the child does not need the funds for college, or decides not to attend a traditional school, the cash value can be used for other opportunities. Those opportunities could include business ventures, income property, or any investments of their choosing. My Million Dollar

Baby plan provides much more flexibility and favorable tax and financial treatment.

In terms of legacy wealth, let's assume that Samantha and Dan start a plan at $100 per month for Dan Jr. at age 5. Over the years, they make a modest $25 increase in their monthly contribution. In 20 years, Dan Jr. would have over $100,000 available for any purpose he would like. If Dan Jr. choses to allow the account to continue to grow, he would be projected to have well over $1,000,000 tax-free cash value before reaching retirement age. In addition, he would be projected to leave close to $2,000,000 to the next generation, thus creating multi-generational millionaires! See the chart below.

As you can see, the My Million Baby concept has the potential to change the trajectory of one's family tree and legacy.

IT'S OK TO START WITH TERM

It's not where you start but where you finish that counts.
—ZIG ZIGLAR

Allow me to introduce you to one final client. This client experienced a very successful career in corporate America. He received many promotions early on. He had been earmarked as an individual expected to climb the corporate ladder, ultimately reaching the top executive level. However, this young man caught the entrepreneur bug and resigned from his corporate management position. Many people, including family and friends, questioned his decision because he had a very young family. His family included his college sweetheart, who gave him her total support, and four young children. Furthermore, his lovely wife was a stay-at-home mom, which was a decision they made together even though they knew that it would be a challenge financially. Ultimately, they had no regrets.

This gentleman, like Mr. Baker, knew the concepts presented to you in this book. He absolutely wanted an indexed universal life policy. In fact, he wanted a premium financed plan that I have presented in this bonus chapter. In addition, he understood that he needed at least $1,000,000 of life insurance coverage in case something happened to him. This would allow his family to maintain their lifestyle without financial hardship in the event of his untimely death.

Here's the problem...he could not afford to buy an indexed universal life insurance policy with a large enough death benefit to meet his true needs. This was quite a dilemma for him because he wanted the very best policy. So, he decided to buy a much cheaper term policy that would give him the appropriate amount of life insurance and fit into his budget. In over ten years, he systematically converted his term policy into an indexed universal life policy as his budget permitted. This client's name is Tony Jackson. Yes, this is my story!

WHAT KIND OF INSURANCE SHOULD YOU HAVE?

I have found over the years that getting some people to change their views on whether they should have term life or whole life insurance can be like trying to get them to change religions. It's very difficult. Some people are very adamant that they should only buy term life insurance while others feel that term insurance is absolutely the worst type of policy. Then there are those who feel exactly the same way about whole life insurance. It can be a very spirited debate. I certainly understand both sides of the argument.

Here's the reality. Life insurance is not a one-size-fits-all strategy. I disagree with anyone who says you should always buy term life insurance nor do I agree with those who say you should always buy whole life insurance. It depends on why you are purchasing the policy.

Is it for temporary life insurance needs? Is it to supplement your retirement income? Is it to hedge against future income taxes? Is it to protect you against the spend down process? Is it to create generational wealth? These are important questions to be answered. The proper order of priorities when purchasing life insurance is 1) Does it give me the proper amount of life insurance? 2) Does it fit into my budget? and 3) Does the type of life policy fit me given my knowledge and my beliefs? These questions provide a baseline and a simple guide in the life insurance purchase process.

TYPES OF LIFE INSURANCE

Decreasing Term Life - The features include level premium, decreasing coverage amount, and no cash value. Used for financial obligations that decrease over time.

Annual Renewable Term Life – The features include increasing premium, level coverage amount, and no cash value. Used for financial obligations that remain constant for a short period of time.

Level Term Life – The features include level premium, level coverage, and no cash value. Premiums remain level for a fixed time period such as 10, 20 or 30 years. Used for financial obligations that remain constant for a short or intermediate time period.

Whole Life – The features include level premium, level coverage, and cash value. Cash value is set by the insurance company based on its general portfolio performance. Used for long-term obligations such as income needs, estate planning, and death taxes.

Single Premium Whole Life – The features include one single premium payment, level coverage, and cash value. Cash value is set by the insurance company based on its general portfolio performance. Used for long-term obligations such as income needs, estate planning, and death taxes.

Universal Life – The features include level or adjustable premium, level coverage, and cash value. Cash value is based on performance of assets in the insurance company's general fund. Used for long-term obligations such as income needs, estate planning, death taxes, and funding retirement needs.

Indexed Universal Life – The features include level or adjustable premium and coverage amount, and cash value. Cash value is based on performance of an underlying stock index such as the S&P 500 Index with some guaranteed protection against market losses. Used for long-term obligations such as income needs, estate planning, death taxes, and funding retirement needs.

Variable Universal Life – The features include level or adjustable premium and coverage amount, and cash value. Cash value is based on performance of various stock market investment accounts with no protection against market losses. Appropriate for clients with a high risk tolerance. Used for long-term obligations such as income needs, estate planning, death taxes, and funding retirement needs.

I AM YOUR POLICY

You and I have similar purposes in this world.

It is your job to provide food, clothing, shelter, medicine, sundry and other essential items for your loved ones; you do this while I lie in your desk drawer.

I have faith and trust in you. Out of your earnings will come the cost of my upkeep. At times, I may appear to be worthless to you – but some day (and who knows when) you and I will change places.

When you are laid to rest, I will come alive and do your job. I will provide the funds necessary for your final resting place and guarantee that your loved ones will not be burdened. I can also provide food, clothing, shelter, medicine, and other essential items your family will continue to need – just as you are doing now. When your work is done and your afterlife begins, my work will begin. Through me, your hands will carry on and so will your legacy.

Whenever you feel the price you are paying for my upkeep is burdensome, remember that I will do more for you and your family than you ever can do for me.

If you do your part, I will do mine.

Sincerely,

YOUR POLICY

Made in the USA
Columbia, SC
05 November 2022